North West England

Edited by Genya Beeby

 Young**Writers**

First published in Great Britain in 2008 by:
Young Writers
Remus House
Coltsfoot Drive
Peterborough
PE2 9JX
Telephone: 01733 890066
Website: www.youngwriters.co.uk

SB ISBN 978-1 84431 727 1

Foreword

Young Writers' Big Green Poetry Machine is a showcase for our nation's most brilliant young poets to share their thoughts, hopes and fears for the planet they call home.

Young Writers was established in 1991 to nurture creativity in our children and young adults, to give them an interest in poetry and an outlet to express themselves. Seeing their work in print will encourage them to keep writing as they grow, and become our poets of tomorrow.

Selecting the poems has been challenging and immensely rewarding. The effort and imagination invested by these young writers makes their poems a pleasure to enjoy reading time and time again.

Contents

Greenleas Primary School, Wallasey

Helsby Hillside Primary School, Helsby

Ellie Rose Sharkey (9)   37
Billy Young & Max Tonge (9)   37

Holy Family Catholic Primary School, Boothstown
Chloe Richards (10)   37
Shannon Mackey (10)   38
Jake Meaney (10)   38
Thomas Crawford (9)   39
Rebecca Gainer (10)   39
Sophie Castle (9)   40
Georgina Raynor (10)   40
Chloe Cullen (10)   40
Olivia Mae Sullivan (10)   41
Toni Hassan (10)   41
Maissie Lever (10)   42
Jessica Susan Spencer (10)   42
Bethany Hughes (10)   43
Amber Smith (10)   43
Jessica Sackfield (9)   44
Annamay Collier (9)   44
Jade Smith (10)   44
Emily Turnbull (10)   45

Merchant Taylors Boys' Junior School, Crosby
Michael Power (9)   45
Joseph Taylor (9)   45
Sam East (11)   46
Tom Harley (9)   47

Nevill Road Junior School, Bramhall
Samantha Ridgway (9)   47
Luke Boardman (9)   47
George William Millership (9)   48
Marcie Fantom (9)   48
Tara Davies (9)   48
Amber Oakes (9)   49
Baylee Ellen Newton (8)   49
Liam Casey (8)   49
Harry Doyle (9)   50
William Sparrow (9)   50
Georgia Thorpe (9)   50

Luke Binyon (8)	51
Rebecca Lyon (9)	51
Kayla Mullings (9)	51
Louise Baxandall (9)	52
Jade Hollick (9)	52
Luke Martin Thomas & Alex Chamberlain (11)	53
Leahanna Jones (9)	53
Eman Buttar & Rosie Callan (11)	54
Meedia Abid (9)	54
Lottie Needham (9)	55
Devon Whetter (9)	55
Ciaran Doyle (11)	56
Lee Rossiter & Callum Williamson (11)	56
Toby White & Jack Higgins (11)	57
Dominic Ciolfi (11)	57
Natasha Izzard (11)	58
Olivia Ellison (9)	58
Lucas Lee (10)	59
Ryan Ellison (10)	59
Noor Buttar (8)	60
Teona Maybury (8)	60

Nine Tree Primary School, Stockbridge Village

Chloe Buck (10)	61
Charlie Jade Wilton (8)	61
Hannah Mitchell (9)	62
Rachel Moffatt (9)	62

Portland Primary School, Birkenhead

Natasha Burns (9)	63

St George's CE Primary School, Heaviley

Oliver Luke Mitchell-Shaw (7)	63
James Ledger (9)	63
Bethany Jones (9)	64
Lois White (9)	64
Amy Worth (9)	64
Lewis Parker (9)	65
Katie Sandford (8)	65
Chloe James (8)	65
Natasha Harford (8)	66

Tyler Barker (9)   66
Nathan Hackney (8)   67
Jordan Metcalfe (9)   67
Nathan Foster (8)   67
Daniella Kinsey (9)   68
Kyle McKinney (9)   68
Daisy May Byrne (8)   69
Alan Penney (9)   69

St Vincent's RC Primary School, Penketh
Michael Byrne (10)   70
Georgia Jones-Bale (10)   70
Joseph Moon (11)   71
Emma Cooney (10)   71
James Cullen (10)   71
Olivia Guy (11)   72
Alice Durell (11)   72
Harry Park (11)   73
Thomas Lawrenson (10)   73
Monica May Nencini (9)   73
Katie Garvey (11)   74
Juliet Porter (10)   74
Rachael Keoghan (10)   74
Michael Manning (11)   75
Alice Clarke (10)   75
Olivia Rudkin (11)   76
Callum Teeling (10)   76
Jordan Matthew Newall (10)   77
Tilly Hemsley (10)   77
Emily Moriarty (11)   78
Hayley Houghton (10)   78
Jack Lavan (11)   79
Jessica Alexander (9)   79
Josh Newton (10)   80
Rubie Maiy Edgar (11)   80
Alex Buckley (11)   81

St Wilfrid's CE Primary School, Grappenhall
Imogen Walker (9)   81
Lara Flannery (10)   81
Hannah Jackson (10)   82

Nicola Hilton (9)	82
Ruby Jude Kelly (8)	82
Charlotte Capper (10)	83
Katie Butler (9)	83
Liam Gray (9)	83
Megan Dunbavand (10)	84
Cameron McLay (9)	84
Charlotte Day (9)	84
Matt Barker (10)	85
Jacob Wilkinson (10)	85
Darcey Brooks (9)	85
Jodie Williams (11)	86
Daniel Evans (10)	86
Lucy Bennison (10)	87
Cameron Elizabeth Nyland (8)	87
Maddie Hardern (8)	88
Olivia Thompson (9)	88
Jacob Mark Nolan (10)	89
Rosie Walton Ryder (10)	89
Sarah Hewitt (10)	90
Maddie Smetham (9)	90
Olivia Lloyd (10)	91
Lydia Marrable (9)	91
Jessica Street (9)	92
Eve Johnstone (10)	92
Lucy Massey (9)	93
Millie Johnson (7)	93
Jimmy Ashcroft (9)	94
Simon Roberts (9)	94
Ross McKinnon (10)	95
Nicole Kelly (9)	95
Rebecca Mitchell (10)	96
Henry James Simpson (9)	96
Eleanor Pink (10)	96
Libby Richardson (7)	97
Isobel McGann (10)	97

Woodchurch Road Primary School, Oxton

Kyle Reed (10)	98
Isabel Nolan (10)	98
Olivia Hulmston (10)	98

Georgina Bryan-Owens (10)	99
Christopher Chan (10)	99
Kyle Burgess (10)	99
Ewan Nolan (8)	100
Ewan McVey (10)	100
Shaun Jones (10)	100
Ashley Kay (10)	101
Nathan Boult (9)	101
Chantelle Davies (10)	101
Summer Gleave (7) & Gabrielle Pritchard (8)	102
Cerys Owen (8)	102
Luke Price (9)	102
Connor Weston (9)	103
Emma Langhorn (9)	103
Rebekah Jane Smith (10)	103
Jessica Jones (10)	104
Ellen Allinson	104
Olivia Asterley (10)	104
Emily Norris (9)	105
Thomas Wynne (10)	105
Chloe Griffiths (8)	106
Suzie Gray (10)	106
Joseph McGeoch (10)	106
Alex Price (9)	107
Ashley Dempsey (10)	107
Lara Jones (10)	107
Clark Isaac Morton (10)	108
Casey Stanley (10)	108

Woodlands Primary School, Formby

Eleanor Gray (10)	109
Henry Thomas Evans (9)	109
Jessica Howlett (10)	110
Lauren MacGregor (9)	110
Alexander Uffendell (9)	111
Lois Diane Hardman (9)	112

The Poems

Poacher, Poacher

Poacher, poacher,
Stalks the night.
Poacher, poacher,
Sets his sight.
Poacher, poacher,
No chance to fight.
Poacher, poacher,
Stalks the night.

Foxes, foxes,
Flash through the night.
Foxes, foxes,
Fast as light.
Foxes, foxes,
Poachers in sight.
Foxes, foxes,
Cannot fight.

Poachers, poachers,
Eyes on the prize.
Poachers, poachers,
Try to guess the size.
Poachers, poachers,
Are big thugs,
Poachers, poachers,
Making rugs.

Oliver Gee & Louise Stanley (11)
Bradley Green Primary School, Hyde

Litter

L ong polluting
I n many streets
T ime to stop
T ime to break the habit
E very time you drop litter
R abbits and other animals can get injured.

Rebecca Stefan (11) & Junior Bennett (10)
Bradley Green Primary School, Hyde

Bears

Bears, bears run free,
To get out of misery.

Bears, bears dancing all the time,
Lots of people say it's not a crime.

Bears, bears caught in a trap,
When they dance people clap.

Bears, bears they won't hurt you,
It's hard to say the things people do.

Bears, bears the day's almost done,
Now your owner's rich, he thinks this is fun.
Bears, bears we will help
And in the end there will be no need to yelp.

Ben Graham (11)
Bradley Green Primary School, Hyde

Why Make Bears Dance?

Why make bears dance?
All they do is run and prance.
They are just weighed down with a chain,
But just think of all their pain.
All they do is just gaze
So please don't make them run round like they are in a maze.
How do you owners cope?
All the bears do is just mope.
How do you think they feel without a great big meal?
So on the count of three,
Let's set the bear free!

Megan Bancroft (11)
Bradley Green Primary School, Hyde

The War

War, war it's all the same
It's just one big awful game
It's all the same we fight to death
Instead of being charged with theft
We fight in the streets
We fight in the air
We fight in the desert
We fight everywhere
People die all over the world
It breaks people's hearts to lose their loved ones
Land is destroyed and people flee
As the enemy laugh with glee.

Andrew Ashall (11) & Chris Chapman (10)
Bradley Green Primary School, Hyde

Held To Dance Against My Will

Where am I?
Why am I here?
Why is there a tag pinned to my ear?
I have been abused,
Poked and struck,
I want to run in front of a truck.
They made me run and prance,
What if I made them dance?
I never get a little treat,
All I get is a handful of wheat.
My owner tied me to a tree,
Just because I didn't dance with glee.

Jake Monks (10)
Bradley Green Primary School, Hyde

Elephant's Interview

Elephant, elephant, what can you see?
Weird people staring at me.
Elephant, elephant, what would you be?
I want to be a bee, small to fit in a tree.
Elephant, elephant, what do you feel?
I feel never to be free to be that bee
Elephant, elephant, what would it be like?
It would be a pleasure being in that tree
I wish it could be me.
Please set me free.

Chloe Parker (10) & Rionna Heathcote (11)
Bradley Green Primary School, Hyde

Recycle

R ecycle please
E mpty bottles
C racked wine glasses
Y ou may cause a crisis
C rushed Coke bottles
L ots of bottles on the floor
E mpty the right bottles into the right bins!

Faye Rebekah Worsell (10)
Bradley Green Primary School, Hyde

Cruelty To A Little Dog

I saw my owner coming near
My feet trembled with fear
Would it be a kick,
A punch or a slap?
All of a sudden I found a cat flap.
I escaped from a hole in the door,
Hunger burned more and more.

Terrie Phillips (10)
Bradley Green Primary School, Hyde

Panda, Panda

Panda, panda you're enraged,
Sitting lonely in a cage.
Panda, panda getting fat,
Oh what you'd do for a pat.
Losing colour, losing hope,
I wonder how you cope.
Panda, panda in the blackness
Oh what you'd do to escape the darkness.

Lewis Wrigley (11)
Bradley Green Primary School, Hyde

Better Place

The world would be a better place,
Right now it is a big disgrace,
In the forest the trees are getting cut down,
We will lose a lot of oxygen, it makes me want to frown,
Poverty makes me feel really bad,
Some people are very mad.

It would be a better place,
If trees would be left alone
And they should get rid of telephones.

Liam Langford (11)
Broadgreen Primary School, Old Swan

Rainforests

Rainforests are getting cut down,
So stop and turn my frown around.

People are cutting down the trees
And I think that is very mean,
So come on and give the rainforest a chance.

Scott Cadwallader (10)
Broadgreen Primary School, Old Swan

Environment

Poverty makes me really sad,
It makes me feel so bad.
Rainforests being cut down
Really does give a frown.
The world could be a better place,
But now it's a big disgrace.
Pollution in the rivers
Gives me the shivers.
Rich people should donate some money
Because it's not that funny.

Roxzi Flynn (11)
Broadgreen Primary School, Old Swan

Recycle

To recycle is a must
Or our world will go bust
Recycle glass, paper and tins
C'mon - fill up your wheelie bins

It only takes a short time to do
So let's start it now, that's me and you
It's up to us; the human race
To make our world a greener place.

Rachael Fisher (9)
Broadgreen Primary School, Old Swan

Gorillas In The Jungle

Jungle drums beat through the Congo,
Deep in the rainforest of Africa
Gorillas beat their chests,
Go green, recycle, look after the planet
Or there won't be any left.

Shaun Phoenix (10)
Broadgreen Primary School, Old Swan

Litter

Litter, litter everywhere,
Some people just don't care.
Bins come in different shapes and sizes,
Colours and even surprises.
There are street cleaners that go sweep, sweep, sweep,
Whoops! What's that on my feet?
One bin's for bottles and one for cans,
One's for sticky food that pongs.
Sort your rubbish and learn to recycle
Otherwise the world won't survive.
Bottles, paper, sweet wrappers, cans,
Crisp packets just fall out of your hands,
Just don't forget to wash your hands.
Baby shoes fall out of the prams,
Mind that dog dirt - I know I will.

Sarah Coyne (10)
Broadgreen Primary School, Old Swan

Save Our World!

We all need to recycle and not drop litter,
People who do that are very, very bitter.
From bags to boxes,
To bottles and cans,
It's getting worse from the pollution off vans.
To save the world we can all do our bit,
Like getting a bottle and recycling it.
Rubbish is all over the floor
And people are throwing more and more.
Please, please this is all I ask,
It is only one little task,
This is all I need you to do,
Is that you start to recycle too!

Abbie Williams (10)
Broadgreen Primary School, Old Swan

Our World

In poor countries people are dying from disease,
Give them vaccinations please oh please.
In our forests deforestation is a problem,
Trees give us oxygen to breathe, so save them.
Animals are dying from our pollution,
We really can't be messing round with evolution.
Being homeless is very bad,
Save homeless people from being sad.
Walking down the street, litter is in the way,
If we don't pick it up the Earth will pay.

Ellie Finnigan (10)
Broadgreen Primary School, Old Swan

Litter

My poem is about litter
And I am feeling very bitter.
As littler is all around us
And can hurt the animals that surround us.
The world would look a lot fitter
If we did not drop litter and put it in the bin
So that wild animals don't lose their limbs.
The world would look a lot cleaner
And would make the world much greener.

Jason Godfrey (10)
Broadgreen Primary School, Old Swan

Recycling And Littering!

You shouldn't ever litter
You should always recycle
We can make it better
If you don't litter
So keep on recycling
Make the world a better place for everyone.

Courtney Fenlon (10)
Broadgreen Primary School, Old Swan

Recycle Now

When you recycle you are using something that has been recycled
which means you can help the world.

The three words when you recycle are reduce, reuse, recycle.
It is silly because there are only some people that recycle
and everyone should help save the world.

I think that we should make a plan and everyone should follow it
and make the world a better place
so start recycling now and save the world.

So recycle now!

Meagan Stephanie Eyres (11)
Broadgreen Primary School, Old Swan

Environment Warning

Litter, litter what is it worth?
I'll tell you what it's worth, it's worth the Earth.

Recycling, that's an idea,
Maybe with this our street will be clear.

Pollution definitely needs to stop,
Otherwise the world will turn to slop.

So listen people everywhere,
Do something to help and show that you care.

Leonne Elizabeth Thompson (11)
Broadgreen Primary School, Old Swan

War Is Hell

I think war is hell because people die.
I think war is hell because people say 'bye-bye' (sometimes forever!)
I think war is hell because people kill.
I know war is hell because people write their will.

Declan Lord (10)
Broadgreen Primary School, Old Swan

Environment

Stop the pollution
Stop the litter
But the most important thing is
Respect for the world.

Stop throwing litter
Just put it in the bin
Really it's only a tin
Just do it.

This needs to stop
The world is turning
It's going the wrong way
If we don't stop it will be the end of the day.

Ross Anthony Dalton (11)
Broadgreen Primary School, Old Swan

Save The Planet

We need to start recycling
We're ruining the Earth
Stop throwing things away
You don't know what they're worth.

There's people on the street
With nowhere to go
Not even a penny
Instead of happy they're low.

We're cutting down the trees
It's called deforestation
We're messing up the world
It's bad for our nation.

Olivia Fowler (11)
Broadgreen Primary School, Old Swan

Litter, Litter

Litter, litter everywhere, all over the streets
Litter, litter here and there, never any for keeps
Make sure you keep the rules
Like clean up the stuff that your dog does
Litter, litter, why?
Don't you care that our streets are ruined?
Litter, litter, what's there to beware?
Chewing gum, crisp packets,
Coke cans and cartons.
Litter, litter, stop it all
Litter, litter, before we fall
Poverty is very bad
Poverty makes me really sad.

Antonia Sim (11)
Broadgreen Primary School, Old Swan

Environment Changes

Climate change is bad for animals
The polar bears don't have much ice
They can't play around
This is horrible and not nice.

Litter is everywhere
Litter should really go into the bins
Fish get wrapped up in it
And some lose their fins.

Pollution is in the sea water
Pollution is very bad
I don't like pollution
When I think about it I'm sad.

Leah Miller (10)
Broadgreen Primary School, Old Swan

A Better Place

A better place would be . . .
Where there's no wars and people get on,
Where there's no cars and there is no pollution,
Where there's no poverty.

A better place would be . . .
Where people don't cut down so many trees,
Where people reduce, reuse, recycle,
Where people don't build things that don't matter.

A better place would be . . .
For you to get a couple of friends
And help the world and tell more people,
Could that be you?

Sarah-Marie Cubbon-Sancto (11)
Broadgreen Primary School, Old Swan

Litter

Litter, litter everywhere and not a place to think.

Litter on the streets, ignored,
Litter in the bins, hold your nose,
Litter in the landfills, just keep filling,
Litter in the world, ignored.

If we recycled what would the world be like?
Clean?
Happy?
Good?
Super!

Phoebe Riley (11)
Broadgreen Primary School, Old Swan

Earth Today

Litter being dropped on the floor,
It's so bad it should be against the law.
Litter is polluting the air,
To look after it just give it some care.

Poverty makes me feel so sad,
But after all it's really bad.
People getting killed in war
And ending up very sore.

Trees being cut down,
To make new stuff in the town.
If you see someone littering tell a cop
And after that hopefully they'll stop!

Mark Saunders (10)
Broadgreen Primary School, Old Swan

I Wish

I wish the world was better,
I wish the world was clean,
If I had my say I would make the world a better place,
Litter, litter, see it everywhere,
I really think it's terrible,
Why don't people care?
People are disrespectful, I don't know why,
If I could choose they would die.
The police should do something about it,
But they're too lazy.

Michael Rodney (10)
Broadgreen Primary School, Old Swan

Climate Poem

The world would be a better place
If there was no pollution
Hurry up you stupid nut
And make a solution
Rubbish, litter everywhere
But some people just don't care
All the trees are getting cut down
And the leaves are getting dirty brown.

Michael O'Neill (10)
Broadgreen Primary School, Old Swan

Litter Is Bad

L itter is bad
I t causes more pollution
T his is a bad thing
T he world needs to be clean
E veryone should help
R emember to recycle.

Sian Warrilow (10)
Broadgreen Primary School, Old Swan

Earth

E veryone can recycle
A t any time
R educe, reuse, recycle
T ell everyone
H ave a heart.

Philip Donton (10)
Broadgreen Primary School, Old Swan

Green

No green would be mean
Rainforest please.
Stop throwing waste in our seas
What can we do to make it green?

Cars rock, I know
But they are destroying the snow
Let's get started
Go! Go! Go!

The world would be a better place
If we didn't have a car race
Eco-friendly would be great
Let's make a poverty mate.

Kids are dying
Mothers are crying
Stop planes flying
The world was full of pollution
Now we've found a solution.

Jake Moorcroft (11)
Broadgreen Primary School, Old Swan

Poverty And Pollution

Poverty is very bad
Poverty is very sad
People have no money
It isn't very funny.

Pollution in the river
Really makes me quiver
It is really bad
It makes me very sad.

Georgia Cullen (10)
Broadgreen Primary School, Old Swan

War!

A horrifying thing is war,
It causes disaster and pain.
It can drive you insane,
People dying,
Loved ones crying.
You can hear gunshots,
Secret plots.
The sadness of the families,
Hopes and dreams,
A thought it seems.
However, it won't last forever,
But only one can win.
So let's work together to stop wars,
War is a sin.
Maybe one day there will be no wars
And all will be fine,
Let's make a new day
Where war is far away in time.

Emma Watts (11)
Greenleas Primary School, Wallasey

Living On The Street

Living on the street
Takes a lot away from you,
No one to love,
Just everyone passing through.

Living on the street,
Nothing else to lose,
Ask people or not,
What would you choose?

Living on the street,
See a sign ahead,
I think it's pointing that way,
A nice warm bed!

Owen Luke Cross (9)
Greenleas Primary School, Wallasey

Wartime

War is cruel,
They are fools,
Lots of gunshots,
No pans or pots.

Long war,
When a man knocks on the door,
It's a death-hole,
But no one is expected to gain their goal.

The sound of cries
When somebody dies,
Sometimes war is for pride,
While somebody died . . .

War is cruel,
They are fools,
Lots of gunshots,
No pans or pots.

Sam Corri (11)
Greenleas Primary School, Wallasey

War Is . . .

War is bad
War is sad
War is death
War is destruction
War is forgettable
War is only bad when you lose!
War is good
War is happy
War is life
War is pleasant
War is unforgettable
War is only good when you win!

William Jones (10)
Greenleas Primary School, Wallasey

Don't Drop It, Bin It,
Don't Bin It, Recycle It!

Don't drop it,
Bin it,
Don't bin it,
Recycle it!

If you drop litter,
Then you're looking very bitter,
So pick up that can, it's very grim
And put it in that rubbish bin!

Take it out of there,
As it's not really fair,
It can go far,
If it's turned into a car,
Recycle it!

Litter looks messy,
It smells bad too,
So don't drop your litter,
As the floor is not a filter!

So don't drop it on the floor,
Or hide it in a bin,
The only thing to do
Is to recycle it!

Caroline Duncan (11)
Greenleas Primary School, Wallasey

Recycling

Recycling, recycling, why should we recycle?
Recycling, recycling, because it is important.
Recycling, recycling, why is it important?
Recycling, recycling, to help save our planet.
Recycling, recycling, recycle please.
Recycling, recycling, save our planet.

Megan Foley (10)
Greenleas Primary School, Wallasey

Poverty Street

Raining, pouring,
Suffering, mourning,
A normal day in Poverty Street.
Money has gone,
For everyone,
Just an average day.

Low on food,
Strangers intrude,
A normal day in Poverty Street.
Hungry, moaning,
Starving, groaning,
Just an average day.

No need for crying,
Everyone's trying
To change the world today.
Now go to bed
And rest your head,
For hope is on its way.

George Booth (11)
Greenleas Primary School, Wallasey

War

War is bad - war is mean
War is dangerous as I've seen
Sitting there sobbing tears
As my heart works its way through all my fears.
Just a scary day.

War is scary - war is terrifying
War is frightening as I've seen
Sitting there sobbing tears
As my heart works its way through all my fears.
Just a scary day.

Bethany Jane Newcombe (11)
Greenleas Primary School, Wallasey

War!

War is bad
War means hate
War is sad
War means death.

Scared, homeless,
Hurt, burnt, orphans,
- *Alone.*

Nobody likes guns,
Nobody likes bombs,
Nobody likes death.

Families separated,
Split apart,
Never to meet again.

Every day there is a war going on
And every day families are dying . . .
Dying . . . dying.

Kay Bain (10)
Greenleas Primary School, Wallasey

Homeless

Some people are homeless,
Not like you and me.
Some people starve,
Not like you and me.
Some places have dirty water,
We don't, not us.
We are lucky in the world,
Not like some places.
We get what we want,
Some people don't, they can't.

Lucy Chittick (10)
Greenleas Primary School, Wallasey

War

War can kill
War can destroy
War can confuse
War can scare
War can tear someone's life.

War is bad
War is sad
War is death
War is loss
War can break someone's heart.

War means fire
War means bombing
War means separation
And that's the way the war goes on.

James Betts (11)
Greenleas Primary School, Wallasey

Animals/Extinction

Tigers, elephants,
Orang-utans too,
Don't kill these animals
They're harmless to you.

Dolphins and whales,
Sharks and loads more,
These animals are crying out
Don't kill any more.

One day there is going to be none left
If people keep killing them,
Please stop killing animals,
We love them.

Emily Currie (10)
Greenleas Primary School, Wallasey

Be Careful With Your Litter

What's that creeping across the ground?
Oh my, it's litter!
The wind's gone up and it's in the air,
It's bad, it's litter,
It's been dropped by someone who doesn't care,
It's wrong, it's litter,
Just put it in the bin
And then there'll be no more litter.
But wait, are we doing the right thing
To some of this litter?
You can reduce it, reuse it
And then recycle it.
So make a difference for the world
With all of your litter.
Do the right thing and don't forget
To be careful with your litter.

Amy Davies (10)
Greenleas Primary School, Wallasey

Into The War

When you go into war,
You will never believe your eyes,
As you try to find some shelter,
You watch many people die.

Altogether with your family,
You hide with your invisible food called 'nothing',
While you can hear painful screams
You can tell that people are suffering.

Rough, dark and evil, that's a war,
But hope is believed,
The war is nearly over,
Then and only then we will be relieved.

James Evans (11)
Greenleas Primary School, Wallasey

Leave Them Where They Are

Please don't make the grass go yellow
Please don't make the trees fall down
Oh please don't take the hedges away
So just leave them where they are.

Now please don't turn the sky to grey
Now please don't turn the oceans green
Oh please don't turn the seas marshy
So just leave them how they are.

Please don't make the hedgehogs hide
Please don't make the badgers scared
Oh please don't make the rabbits rare
So just leave them where they are.

Now please don't turn pondweed brown
Now please don't turn dragonflies quiet
Now please don't make frogs bite their tongues
So just please leave them how they are.

Olivia Hogg (10)
Greenleas Primary School, Wallasey

Does It Make A Difference? No!

Does it matter if we're black or white?
Does it really need to cause a fight?
All the people, black and white,
Should stand hand in hand and reunite.

Racism causes bullying and fights,
But does it matter if we're black or white?
It's only a colour, not your life,
And you should be happy, black or white!

Racism should stop!
It's really unkind,
So please stop racism,
It's not worth a fight!

Emily Thompson (11)
Greenleas Primary School, Wallasey

War Kills!

Gunshots fire,
Echoing through the air,
Bang!
People are dying.

The lucky ones survive,
They start crying,
Bang!
People are dying.

The last shot is fired,
The last man standing,
Bang!
People are dying.

The air is quiet,
All you can hear is gunshots in the distance,
Bang!
People are dying.

Alex Johnson (11)
Greenleas Primary School, Wallasey

War Cries Heard Today

War cries heard today,
War cries from miles away,
'Cause war will be coming soon,
And be ready, death is on its way.

War cries nearer today,
War cries from not so far away,
'Cause war will be coming very soon,
And be ready, for death is on its way.

War cries here today,
War cries right here, nowhere away,
'Cause war has come
And we weren't ready
For death has come upon us.

Marc John Simmons (11)
Greenleas Primary School, Wallasey

Being Homeless

Cold, scared, heartbroken,
That is how they feel.
Shivering, motionless, desperate for help,
That is how they feel.
Hard, sharp, imagine sleeping under a bridge,
That is how they feel.
Shivering, motionless, desperate for help,
That is how they feel.
Cold, scared, heartbroken,
That is how they feel.
Torn, ripped, these are your clothes,
That is how they feel.
Hard, sharp, imagine sleeping under a bridge,
That is how they feel.
Shivering, motionless, desperate for help,
That is how they feel.
Cold, scared, heartbroken,
That is how they feel -
Always!

Kimberley Roberts (11)
Greenleas Primary School, Wallasey

Extinction

Today's the day the animals get revenge
'Cause if you go in the woods to eat your pie
All the trees and stuff will be gone
And turned into a waste.
You're killing Mother Nature
It's really bad
The world's losing health
It's really sad
It's wrong so do your bit
Now, right now.

Sabrina Marnell (10)
Greenleas Primary School, Wallasey

Recycle

R ecycle
E ncourage other people to recycle
C artridges for ink can be recycled
Y our aluminium cans can be recycled
C ardboard can be recycled
L ove your town and take care of the . . .
E nvironment

Please, please, please take care of the environment
And reduce . . . reuse . . . recycle.

Josh Bartlett (11)
Greenleas Primary School, Wallasey

Poverty

Loads of people have no home
But all the people do not moan
They don't even have any toys to play with
And they also don't have an oven to bake with
They are all starving
And still never carving
And it's just like another world
Please help!

Megan Gwilliams (10)
Greenleas Primary School, Wallasey

Recycling

R emember to recycle
E ncourage others to recycle
C ardboard can be recycled
Y ou'll give us a big help, if you recycle
C ould you recycle all your life?
L earn how good it is to recycle
E veryone should do their bit.

Robert Allanson (10)
Greenleas Primary School, Wallasey

Does It Matter?

Does it matter what colour skin we have
Or how old you are?
Does it matter if you are able-bodied or disabled?
The answer is . . . *no!*

It is all our world,
So let us live in harmony,
It does not matter if we are strong or weak,
It only matters that we live together in peace.
It does not matter if you are famous or not,
If you are on television or just watching it,
We are all just as important as each other.

Does it matter if you are scruffy or smart
Or if you are tall or small?
Does it matter if you are rich or poor,
The answer is . . . *no!*

Caleb Holliday (10)
Greenleas Primary School, Wallasey

Rainforests, Why? Why?

Why? Why? Should rainforests die?
Why? Why? Should rainforests try?
Why? Why? Do we burn down trees?
I beg you, stop it, please!

Why? Why? Should animals suffer?
Why? Why? Should animals scutter?

Why? Why? Do we destroy rainforests
And all the things in them?
That's my question.
Stop!

Mia Franco (9)
Greenleas Primary School, Wallasey

Why, Why?

Why, why?
Why do people make the rainforest cry?
Hurt the animals, make them die?
Don't be shy!
Speak up, say no,
Come on, let's go!

Why, why?
No matter how we try,
They will not stop,
Until every tree drops.
Destroying beautiful places,
All the animal races.

Why, why?
Don't stop to sigh,
Greedy, horrible, unfair,
They don't want to share.
But never give up hope,
On this endless slope.

Why, why?
Life is like a pie,
You can have too much,
Hands off, don't touch!
Even though it's great,
Perhaps it's too late.

Why, why?
Reach for the sky,
Come on, let's fly
So let's . . .
Help the rainforest!

Becky Moulsdale (10)
Greenleas Primary School, Wallasey

War Is Here!

War is here,
Beware, beware,
War is here,
Look out! It could be anywhere!

War is here,
Cannons at the ready,
War is here,
Sergeants are steady!

War is here,
Hide away,
War is here,
It could be any day!

War is here,
Children on the train,
War is here,
Soldiers feel the pain!

War is here,
The bombs are let,
War is here,
That's a big threat!

Careful, careful,
You could be hurt any minute,
Careful, careful,
Before you're hit!

At last, war is over,
Let's celebrate
And live our happy lives.

Jodie Oliver (10)
Greenleas Primary School, Wallasey

War

Bomb! Bomb!
Everyone's screaming
Gun! Gun!
People are fleeing.

People are running to the Anderson shelter
At the bottom of the garden
Clear from any danger.

The air raid alarm is ringing
Throughout my ears,
So loud it could deafen anyone
In a split second.

Bang! Houses are destroyed.
People are dead.
They are all waiting for people
To come out from underneath the rubble
. . . Alive!

The army troops are dying
All around the world,
How do we help them?
Pray, pray and pray some more.
They will thank us for evermore.

Five years later
It has all stopped,
Some people return home
And some people do not.

Hannah Bromley (10)
Greenleas Primary School, Wallasey

The Bomb

Listen to the sounds
People are screaming
Listen to the sounds
Children are crying
Listen to the sounds
People are dying
Listen to the sounds
There are none, it's all gone.

Libby Whittle (10)
Greenleas Primary School, Wallasey

Recycle!

Recycle, reduce
Reuse more things.
To make people more pleased.
Save paper, cardboard and glass
To make people more pleased.
If you don't recycle
The world won't be pleased.

James Knipe & Lee Preston (9)
Helsby Hillside Primary School, Helsby

Untitled

Don't, don't, don't chop the trees down,
Not in the rainforest you won't.
Hear the beautiful noise of birds
Singing in the sunlight.
Don't, don't, don't catch animals too
And torture them like some people do.

Louise Henderson & Sophie Henderson (9)
Helsby Hillside Primary School, Helsby

Bins, Boxes And Bags

No to rubbish
Bad for the world
Makes you feel sad
Watching the world go mad

Tins and jars
Are taken by cars
And turned into useful stuff

No to rubbish
Bad for the world
Makes you feel sad
Watching the world go mad

Recycle as much as you can
Here comes the green bin
Nappies, clothes and lots more stuff
Are things that can go in

No to rubbish
Bad for the world
Makes you feel sad
Watching the world go mad

In the garden is everything green
When you put things in the brown bin
You are making the garden green

No to rubbish
Bad for the world
Makes you feel sad
Watching the world go mad

Newspapers are full of ink
When you put them in the green bag
They will be gone in a flash of a blink

No to rubbish
Bad for the world
Makes you feel sad
Watching the world go mad

Bottles and plastic
Go in the box that is red
When you close it
Don't bang your head

No to rubbish
Bad for the world
Makes you feel sad
Watching the world go mad.

Kate Shingler & Sam Ames (9)
Helsby Hillside Primary School, Helsby

Cutting Down Trees

Cutting down trees
Havoc, destruction to the rainforest
Extinction to habitats.

Ban chainsaws, axes
The forest will never be the same
Recycle paper so no tree shall be destroyed.

Trees are precious to monkeys
Don't farm the land
Let the rainforest live.

Adam Johnson & Tom Gibson (9)
Helsby Hillside Primary School, Helsby

The Air's Nightmare

Pollution! Pollution!
In the smoggy air.
Scientists and people just cannot bare
The North and South Pole suffering
In the caught up sun
And the blazing Earth
Pollution! Pollution!
Do you care?

Rebecca Clement (9)
Helsby Hillside Primary School, Helsby

Recycle More

We need to recycle
Tins, paper and cans
Ride more bicycles
And save the lands

Stop the incinerator
And turn off the lights
Stop throwing paper away
Cut down the number of flights

Turn off the radiator
And recycle the plastic
Turn on the lights later
And recycle that elastic

Stop the incinerator
And turn off the lights
Stop throwing paper away
Cut down the number of flights

Stop the factories
And keep the dams
Recycle more batteries
And save the land.

Stop the incinerator
And turn off the lights
Stop throwing paper away
Cut down the number of flights

Stop global warming
Save the polar bear
The world is amazing
And it needs care!

Stop the incinerator
And turn off the lights
Stop throwing paper away
Cut down the number of flights.

George Houghton (9) & Jacob Sterling (8)
Helsby Hillside Primary School, Helsby

Our World

Putting rubbish in the ponds
Really is the limit,
Cos we still wanna hear
The frogs going *ribbit!*

Our world is the title
And we need to recycle
Come join the recycling crew
Here we make your future
Marvellous for you!

Cutting trees down ruins homes
The birds will die out
And we won't hear their tones
Also trees help the air
And put out oxygen everywhere

Our world is the title
And we need to recycle
Come join the recycling crew
Here we make your future
Marvellous for you!

To the incinerator we say no
Anything that needs burning
Is where it will go!

Our world is the title
And we need to recycle
Come join the recycling crew
Here we make your future
Marvellous for you!

Holly Gemmell & Eve Draper (9)
Helsby Hillside Primary School, Helsby

Recycle!

Glass that we do not smash
We put it in the recycle bin

Recycle here
Recycle there
Recycle everywhere

Plastic that it is sometimes elastic
We put it in the recycle bin

Recycle here
Recycle there
Recycle everywhere

Tins that are metal like pins
We put them in the recycle bin

Recycle here
Recycle there
Recycle everywhere.

Jonathan Cooper (9) & Reuben Shingler (8)
Helsby Hillside Primary School, Helsby

Untitled

Stop the incinerator
Polluting the stunning Earth.
Recycle the paper and help the environment.

Recycle the world
It helps to save nature.

Stop cutting down the trees
And turn off the lights
Cut down on smoking chimneys, stop global warming!

Recycle the world
It helps to save nature!

Jonathan Jones & Petrina Warburton (9)
Helsby Hillside Primary School, Helsby

Green Dream

We're chopping down trees
In the sweltering weather
Oak, palm, willow, holly
We're chopping down trees together
Stop!
Don't!
It's a great green dream!
Every tree deserves to stand
Ash, elm, fire, pine
They should stay on land!

Ellie Rose Sharkey (9)
Helsby Hillside Primary School, Helsby

Recycle Paper

Recycle more rubbish
So we can publish
More paper for our schools
We give the paper
To the creator
And only fools
Can't be bothered to save the world.

Billy Young & Max Tonge (9)
Helsby Hillside Primary School, Helsby

Tread Lightly

Tread lightly for the Earth is our only home,
Tread lightly for the seas are full of foam,
Tread lightly and keep the streets litter-free,
Tread lightly, upon the nights to see,
Tread lightly for we need clean water to live,
Tread lightly for clean water we need to give,
Tread lightly for we need to go green!

Chloe Richards (10)
Holy Family Catholic Primary School, Boothstown

You Can Do Something About It!

Homeless people living on the street
You can do something about it!
Trees being cut down every single day
You can do something about it!
Children dying because they have no clean water
You can do something about it!
People polluting our water and killing wildlife
You can do something about it!
Children being called names because they're not white
You can do something about it!
Poor animals being hurt, just left to die in the dirt
You can do something about it!
People getting a disease and starting to sneeze
You can do something about it!
You do need to help and remember
You can do something about it!

Shannon Mackey (10)
Holy Family Catholic Primary School, Boothstown

Tread Lightly

Tread lightly for the Earth is our responsibility.
Tread lightly for the sun is our light.
Tread lightly for God created the Earth.
Tread lightly for the Earth is being polluted.
Tread lightly for the Earth is going to melt.
Tread lightly for the Earth is getting killed by all the waste
                such as used plastic bottles and cans.
Tread lightly for the Earth should be a happy place.
Tread lightly for the Earth should stay safe.

Jake Meaney (10)
Holy Family Catholic Primary School, Boothstown

Recycle, Recycle

Recycle your plastic
To make it fantastic
Recycle your tins
Don't put them in bins

Recycle your glass
To make it last
Recycle your metal
Even that old kettle

Paper can be used again
Loaded up by the crane
Squashed and pulped into mush
Recycle - it's one big rush.

Thomas Crawford (9)
Holy Family Catholic Primary School, Boothstown

Litter

Throw your litter in the bins,
Except all of your cans and tins,
We can recycle these, that's what we do,
Just to help the world and you!

The world is dying day by day,
Just so that we can have our own way,
Now take your paper, cans and tins,
Off to your local recycling bins.

So remember, throw your litter in the bins,
Except all of your cans and tins.

Rebecca Gainer (10)
Holy Family Catholic Primary School, Boothstown

How To Make The World A Better Place

Look after our beautiful world,
Care for its clear blue skies,
Its colourful flowers blooming in the breeze
And its long winding rivers.
If we looked after the world it would be much clearer
To see what a beautiful world we live in!

The people of the world need to be careful,
We know what could happen.
If we don't buck up soon our world will be like a dying flower patch!

Sophie Castle (9)
Holy Family Catholic Primary School, Boothstown

Tread Lightly

Tread lightly for the echoing voice of a bird is spectacular.
Tread lightly so God's creatures aren't disturbed by Man.
Tread lightly so the mighty mountains can provide a beautiful
                                        and calming atmosphere.
Tread lightly so butterflies can flutter in the wind.
Tread lightly so the tide may come and go unpolluted.
Tread lightly so the daffodils may bloom every year in spring.
Tread lightly so everyone has access to clean water.
Tread lightly so God's world may live in peace and harmony.

Georgina Raynor (10)
Holy Family Catholic Primary School, Boothstown

Tread Lightly

Tread lightly for the Earth is our home.
Tread lightly for the lapping waves of the sea.
Tread lightly for the mighty trees standing tall.
Tread lightly for the magnificent fish in the sea.
Tread lightly so the beautiful flowers can bloom in the springtime.
Tread lightly so the world can live undisturbed.

Chloe Cullen (10)
Holy Family Catholic Primary School, Boothstown

The Natural Bulldozer!

I am an old thrown out bottle,
The world we live in, oh we throttle,
I am being kicked around far, far away,
Hoping I'll be put in a recycling bin one day!

In years to come you'll be full of sorrow,
People dump rubbish like there's no tomorrow,
So if you want to help the world and me,
Try and uncover the eco-friendly key!

We are slowly destroying the world we live in,
This poverty battle one day we'll win,
Litter like me; please clean me up,
Rubbish needs to go in a bin,
Spoiling our world is a terrible sin.

The world is our glorious leader,
It's our magnificent scene feeder,
You're acting like you want to live,
Without the world's natural resources,
The ruining of this Earth is
As strong as the water's fierce forces.

Now this is the end of my appeal,
Do you want to agree on a deal?
I hope you get the message here,
To improve our world year after year!

Olivia Mae Sullivan (10)
Holy Family Catholic Primary School, Boothstown

Litter

L itter is a horrible thing when you throw it about,
I t's killing our environment which is going to rot, no doubt,
T rees are being demolished, just for your paper,
T rees that you see now, you may never see them later.
E verybody should help the environment, in their own special way,
R emember to keep the environment safe, every single day.

Toni Hassan (10)
Holy Family Catholic Primary School, Boothstown

I Dream Of A World

I dream of a world where we live in peace
and flowers grow around me.
I dream of a world where the skies are blue
and the bright green grass surrounds me.
I dream of a world where poverty ends
and the songbirds sing in the cloudless sky.
I dream of a world where all wars end
and the seas sparkle before my eyes.
I dream of a world where we all have clean water
and together as friends join hands.
I dream of a world where all are free
to travel to distant lands.

Maissie Lever (10)
Holy Family Catholic Primary School, Boothstown

Tread Lightly

Tread lightly for the Earth is our home,
Tread lightly on the rippling waves of the sea,
Tread lightly for the field is full of red roses
And the scent of their strong perfume.

Tread lightly for the Earth is our land,
Tread lightly for the river is flowing free,
Tread lightly for the flowers are blooming brightly.

Tread lightly and let the Earth be a loving place,
Tread lightly and not waste the water that gives us life,
Tread lightly for the future is in our hands.

Jessica Susan Spencer (10)
Holy Family Catholic Primary School, Boothstown

Tread Lightly

Tread lightly for the world is our responsibility.
Tread lightly for it's water that helps us live.
Tread lightly for the world is full of possibility.
Tread lightly for the wonderful world God gives.
Tread lightly for the sea is a wonderland.
Tread lightly in a world of endangered creatures.
Tread lightly for the beautiful beaches where your feet
                                    slip through the sand.
Tread lightly for the world is full of exciting features.
Tread lightly for the sun provides us with heat.
Tread lightly for the flowers so colourful and rare.
Tread lightly for the ground beneath our feet.
Tread lightly for the world now needs our care.

Bethany Hughes (10)
Holy Family Catholic Primary School, Boothstown

Footprints

Tread lightly on the Earth which we live upon.
Tread lightly on the flowers that have started to bloom.
Tread lightly on the sand which is like silk.
Tread lightly on the freshly cut grass.
Tread lightly on the sun which shines on us each day.
Tread lightly on the rainforests of evergreen.
Tread lightly on the clashing, wavy, white-tipped sea.
Tread lightly on the waterfalls which tumble and fall.
Tread lightly on the world that we promised God to look after.

Amber Smith (10)
Holy Family Catholic Primary School, Boothstown

Tread Lightly

Tread lightly for the world is in our hands
Tread lightly for the sun that warms our bodies
Tread lightly for the sparkling rivers where we paddle our toes
Tread lightly for the water which quenches our thirst
Tread lightly for the rain that pitter-patters on our heads
Tread lightly for the flowers whose perfume fills our senses
Tread lightly for the trees who give us their shade
Tread lightly for the stars that light our way
Tread lightly on the Earth for future generations.

Jessica Sackfield (9)
Holy Family Catholic Primary School, Boothstown

Tread Lightly!

Tread lightly for the streets are paved with litter,
Tread lightly for our future could be bitter,
Tread lightly for the trees that loom above us,
Tread lightly for the bees that buzz,
Tread lightly for the seas are becoming black,
Tread lightly for the litter should be in a sack,

So this is a poem just to say . . .
Look after our world in every way!

Annamay Collier (9)
Holy Family Catholic Primary School, Boothstown

Recycle, Recycle

R ecycle, recycle it will make an immense difference,
E veryday animals are being killed by litter thrown on the streets!
C limate change needs to stop,
Y ou can reduce your eco footprint.
C hildren die every 15 seconds from dreadful, dirty water!
L oss of plants and trees means we are losing oxygen!
E veryone needs to look after our world!

Jade Smith (10)
Holy Family Catholic Primary School, Boothstown

Pollution!

P olluting the environment around us,
O il leaks and petrol fumes,
L itter shouldn't touch the ground,
L it cigarettes pollute the air,
U nder the sea rubbish lurks,
T in cans roll under bushes,
I f we keep on polluting the environment,
O ur future won't be right.
N ow it's our responsibility to make the world a better place!

Emily Turnbull (10)
Holy Family Catholic Primary School, Boothstown

Pollution, Pollution

Pollution, pollution,
Oh what is the solution?
Walk to work,
(If the weather's not berserk!)
On the street I saw it glitter,
It wasn't gold, it was litter,
It made me feel so bitter.

And a look in a book,
Is way better than a video game,
Remember, don't let the world go up in a flame!

Michael Power (9)
Merchant Taylors Boys' Junior School, Crosby

Pollution

I choke, I choke on all the smoke.
I wheeze, I wheeze, it brings me to my knees.
The oil, the oil it brings turmoil.
The melting icebergs in the west.
Clearly my planet is not at its best.

Joseph Taylor (9)
Merchant Taylors Boys' Junior School, Crosby

The Solution To Pollution

Pollution is in evidence everywhere,
On the ground and in the air,
Up the hills and in the sea,
Pollution is clear to you and me.

Fires burn with a ghastly smell,
Turning the sky to a living hell,
Smoke discolours it, deadly black,
It's getting ever harder to go back.

It billows out of many cars,
Swiftly eliminating the stars,
The sooner we find a different fuel,
The sooner we end this dismal duel.

Pollution even comes from litter,
The scent of it is oh so bitter,
We can fix the problem with incredible ease,
Recycle, and feel a summery breeze.

It turns the sea into a melting pot,
As the world becomes increasingly hot,
The fish die out, the ocean's dry,
But we can fix this, if we try.

The worldwide problem of pollution,
Has a rather easy solution,
Coming up are ways to win,
Ways to beat the eternal sin.

Recycle your rubbish please,
We can do it, I'm not a tease,
Take less plane flights, change your car,
If you do it, you're a star.

Buy Fairtrade, not rainforest paper,
It's not a joke, I'm not a japor,
Ride a bike, or take a hike,
Try it today and see what it's like.
And if we all do work together,
Pollution won't beat us,
Never ever!

Sam East (11)
Merchant Taylors Boys' Junior School, Crosby

Our Environmental World

When I see people flitter their litter,
It's like wasting paper from the forest trees,
They give us oxygen to help us breathe.
Burning coal from our trees, filling our air with disease,
Climate change is bad for the Poles, disappearing like burning coals.
Dropping litter is against the law, people fighting like a war.
Some people don't need poverty, not just like kids with books
of novelty,
When I see people cycling, it makes me feel like recycling.

Tom Harley (9)
Merchant Taylors Boys' Junior School, Crosby

What Will The World Be Like When I Am Forty?

Will the towns be flooded with litter?
Litter here, litter there, litter everywhere!
Will the litter make poisonous gas spread through the air?
Litter here, litter there, litter everywhere!
Will the world be covered in landfill sites because of all the litter?
Litter here, litter there, litter everywhere!

Pick up your litter
And save the world!

Samantha Ridgway (9)
Nevill Road Junior School, Bramhall

What Is The Need Of War?

Is there really a need for war?
You either end up dead or sore.
What's the need for all the dying?
And all the families end up crying.

Do we really want global warming?
You're all getting plenty of warning.

Luke Boardman (9)
Nevill Road Junior School, Bramhall

Shoo!

Dodo, Dodo, where did you go?
Your black beak was always on show.
You hopped around, looking for food,
But when men saw you, you were shooed, shooed, shooed!
The men vowed revenge,
And hurt you till the end,
All for food, the thing you were shooed from,
We found this out on Zoo.com.
But if we were kind and helped the planet,
Dodo, Dodo, could you come back?
Parliament and MPs, could you help
So the tiger, panda, koala need not suffer Dodo's fate,
And end up on our plate?

George William Millership (9)
Nevill Road Junior School, Bramhall

Questions

Do we know what's right and wrong?
Do we know the future?
Do you see the difference?
How old are you now?
Are you suffering badly?
Are the skies still blue or are they dull and grey?
Who do you think you are?

Marcie Fantom (9)
Nevill Road Junior School, Bramhall

Extinct Animals

Animals are becoming extinct because of being hunted.
The number of animals on the Earth is being reduced.
Endangered animals are being hunted for their meat and their horns.
A lot of animals need our help so let's see if you help!

Tara Davies (9)
Nevill Road Junior School, Bramhall

Save Us

Food, meat, it's to beat!
Dolphin swimmers, reptile friends
Farm animals
Gorillas help, gorillas help!
Chubby tigers, they're so cute
Help, help, animals are dying
Save us!
Will these animals be alive?
If you don't help, they might not be.

Amber Oakes (9)
Nevill Road Junior School, Bramhall

Future

Get our future just perfect
We can prove that the world needs to get better
Everyone should be punished. Keep the world healthy.
Save our planet from global warming
Don't drive your car everywhere you go
Save the ozone layer
Don't let the ocean get polluted.

Baylee Ellen Newton (8)
Nevill Road Junior School, Bramhall

Where Were You?

Tree: Where were you when we were cut down?
Tiger: Where were you when I got shot to death?
Monkey: Where were you when my home was destroyed?
Earth: Where were you when my ozone layer was destroyed?

Please save them!

Liam Casey (8)
Nevill Road Junior School, Bramhall

The Three Rs

R educe, reuse, recycle,
E veryone should recycle,
C an you do your best to recycle?
Y ou should recycle,
C arry on recycling,
L earn to recycle,
I recycle,
N early everything can be recycled.
G reat Britain recycles!

Harry Doyle (9)
Nevill Road Junior School, Bramhall

Save The World

Horrid, smelly, yucky litter,
Makes my tongue go so bitter,
If we bought loads more bins,
That would rid us of our sins.

We are cutting down lots of trees,
Which is making lots of fees
From the dreaded Ministry
Of very hateful tyranny.

William Sparrow (9)
Nevill Road Junior School, Bramhall

Save The World

Will there be a house,
food and heating or a bed?

WIll all animals be extinct,
like a dodo and a Tasmanian tiger?

Please stop and think . . .
Can you change the way you are?

Georgia Thorpe (9)
Nevill Road Junior School, Bramhall

Recycle Poem

Ten old newspapers
Nine cans of beans
Eight cans of Coke
Seven old jumpers
Six lots of plastic
Five paper plates
Four old jars
Three plastic tubs
Two old bins
One plastic bottle.

Luke Binyon (8)
Nevill Road Junior School, Bramhall

Recycling

R ecycle
E verything
C arefully.
Y ou should have a recycling bin.
C areful the black bag doesn't rip.
L eave your black bag
I n the recycling centre.
N ever throw rubbish on the floor.
G ive and share to keep the world a better place!

Rebecca Lyon (9)
Nevill Road Junior School, Bramhall

Reduce, Reuse, Recycle

Reduce, reuse, recycle
It makes the world a better place
Reduce, reuse, recycle
That is what the children say
Reduce, reuse, recycle!

Kayla Mullings (9)
Nevill Road Junior School, Bramhall

What Is War?

What is war?
War is bad, war is evil, war is mad.
What is war?
War is mean, a mean machine.
What is war?
It hurts your feelings.
It deletes your homes.
What is war?
It bombs your countries.
It takes your family and your friends.
What is war?
It is not clever, it is not wise.
What is war?
It is annoying.
What is war?
It sends out gas from up high,
Air raid from the sky.
What is war?
It stops you living a happy life.
War, I've had enough of it.

Louise Baxandall (9)
Nevill Road Junior School, Bramhall

Rainforest Is Great!

R ain trickles from the leaves,
A ll sights are green,
I rresistible fresh smells,
N ever eat a slug!
F orests full of trees,
O pen air for me,
R ain is my favourite weather,
E ven if it's wet,
S oaking wet people,
T orrential rain!

Jade Hollick (9)
Nevill Road Junior School, Bramhall

War And Peace

War is dangerous,
War is bad.
War is dangerous,
War is sad.
War is dangerous,
It makes me mad.
War is dangerous,
It took my dad.
War is dangerous,
It's the worst experience
I ever had.

Peace is right,
It stops the fight.
Peace is right,
It leads to light.
Peace is right,
So we sleep tonight.
Peace is right,
It makes for a better sight.
Peace is right, peace is right.

Luke Martin Thomas & Alex Chamberlain (11)
Nevill Road Junior School, Bramhall

Simile Poem

Recycling
Recycling is rubbish
Recycling is cans
Recycling is plastic
Recycling is saving the world
Recycling is jars
Recycling is put in big bins
Recycling is great, try it!

Leahanna Jones (9)
Nevill Road Junior School, Bramhall

Air Pollution

Stop polluting the air,
Since it isn't fair.
Factories and power stations,
Are wrecking our nations.

To get to the bar,
Walk instead of using the car.
Don't sin,
Put rubbish in the bin.
Don't cut down the trees,
'Cause there won't be any breeze.

Do these things,
The brighter future it brings.
Stop pollution,
'Cause it isn't the solution.

Eman Buttar & Rosie Callan (11)
Nevill Road Junior School, Bramhall

Rainforest

R ainforests are pretty places.
A nd come and see all their sad faces.
I n the creatures there lie.
N umbers of creatures will not survive.
F or if you keep it safe and clear
O h the happy noises you will hear.
R ound some corners you'll just listen
E nding to environment will begin.
S adly the forest will shrink.
T o look after the forest you must think.

Meedia Abid (9)
Nevill Road Junior School, Bramhall

Recycling Is Very Strange

Recycling is very strange,
You don't know what you can do,
'Should I put this in
Or straight in the bin?
And what about this thing from the loo?
Ew!'

Recycling is very strange,
And when there's no rubbish to lose?
Well, there's some plastic bags,
But they're practically rags,
So what do I do? *Reuse!*

Recycling is very strange,
So why do we do it anyway?
Well it all adds up
To the amount of floods
That we have in the future day!

Lottie Needham (9)
Nevill Road Junior School, Bramhall

Rainforest Recycling

R ecycle to help the rainforest,
A nything is good,
I n any weather animals suffer,
N othing to help is utter jibberish,
F or the animals of the world,
O nly idiots would cut it down,
R euse before recyling,
E verything counts,
S ave the world,
T he world needs saving, *you* can help.

Devon Whetter (9)
Nevill Road Junior School, Bramhall

My War

I run about the battlefield,
Hoping not to get shot,
I suppose if I am killed right now,
My body will be left to rot.
But if that happened and people in England,
Knew what had happened to me,
I suppose nobody would really be bothered,
Apart from friends and family.
And also children, playing on PlayStations,
Enjoying the blood and gore,
I suppose they don't know what it's really like,
To be fighting in a war.
But it isn't just me suffering,
There are other people by my side,
And innocent citizens of Afghanistan,
Now, they don't feel pride.
So you snuggle up in front of EastEnders!
Don't worry about the world over here!
Have fun in your cotton wool lives,
Don't feel any proper fear.
I don't enjoy fighting, but it's what I do,
To give the world some peace,
Give a thought for just one minute,
One minute, at the least . . .

Ciaran Doyle (11)
Nevill Road Junior School, Bramhall

The Environment

If you want to be cool turn off the switch,
Lands are dirty, the sea is murky.
If you want to be cool turn off the switch,
The cars are running and the petrol's burning.
If you want to be cool turn off the switch,
The pollution's burning and the ice is melting.
If you want to be cool turn off the switch.

Lee Rossiter & Callum Williamson (11)
Nevill Road Junior School, Bramhall

Bang Goes The World!

Trees are falling all around
And people are not bothered.
If we carry on this way,
Bang goes the world!

Heed these words of wisdom,
An ice cap has just melted.
Polar bears can't swim forever,
So splash goes a race.

Bang, bang, bang, bang,
And the guns are being reloaded.
The Earth is getting hotter,
And the sun keeps on expanding.

The fishes will be happy,
But we'll all be dead.
We'll be on the seabed,
With fishes on our heads.

Trees have fallen,
Ice has melted,
The sun is expanding,
Listen to me or,
Boom, crash, smash, bang goes the world.

Toby White & Jack Higgins (11)
Nevill Road Junior School, Bramhall

Litter Is Bad

Litter is bad, don't drop it on the ground,
'Cause then you'll have to pay about sixty pounds.
Litter is bad, don't drop it on the floor,
'Cause then you'll have to pay even more.
Litter is bad for you and the Earth,
Stop dumping now, it's not your turf.
Litter is bad 'cause you'll get caught by a cop,
Bad things will happen, so you may as well stop.

Dominic Ciolfi (11)
Nevill Road Junior School, Bramhall

No More World

No more world,
Animals are slowly dying
And no one seem to be crying.
No more world,
Homes are being destroyed
And people are getting annoyed.
No more world,
Litter on the ground,
There will be no more people around.

No more world,
No more world.

Natasha Izzard (11)
Nevill Road Junior School, Bramhall

10 Green Bottles Sitting On A Log

10 green bottles
 9 cans of Coke.
 8 old newspapers.
 7 glass bottles.
 6 cardboard boxes.
 5 paper sheets.
 4 tin cans.
 3 words - reduce, reuse, recycle.
 2 blue wheely bins.
 1 green wheely bin.

Olivia Ellison (9)
Nevill Road Junior School, Bramhall

War

In war there is lots of bloodshed,
In war lots of people die,
In war there is a lot of killing,
In war I hope I will survive.
War shouldn't happen,
War is a bad thing,
What is proven in war?
In war there is a lot of shouting,
In war there is a lot of gunfire,
In war there is a lot of medals,
In war the tears are shed,
I hope we will survive.

Lucas Lee (10)
Nevill Road Junior School, Bramhall

Green

If you wanna be clean,
Then you've gotta be green.
The land is dirty
And the seas are murky.
If you wanna be clean,
Then you've gotta be green.
If you're gonna pollute,
Then you are the root.
If you wanna be clean,
Then you've gotta be green.

Ryan Ellison (10)
Nevill Road Junior School, Bramhall

The Rubbish Bin

I was walking down the street,
I saw a rubbish bin, it was empty.
And guess what? All the rubbish was all over the ground,
I saw . . .
10 pieces of cardboard all ripped through,
 9 pieces of paper ripped to bits,
 8 plastic bottles all in a row.
 7 glass bottles singing with joy,
 6 glass . . . oh no, people could get hurt,
 5 pieces of wood shiny as gold,
 4 pieces of plastic, 'ow!' that hurts.
 3 lots of metal all muddled up,
 2 plastic bags that people step on
 1 newspaper laying about.

Let's pick them up and put them in the bin
To help the environment.

Noor Buttar (8)
Nevill Road Junior School, Bramhall

Recycling

R ecycling is good,
E veryone can do it, they could.
C ans, Coke bottles, you can recycle them too,
Y ou could recycle all the time.
C ans, bottles, including food but not lemon and lime,
L andfills are full of rubbish that you can recycle.
I nteresting things that you don't want, take them to a charity shop.
N othing will stop you recycling, it's good for the environment.
G lass bottles, you don't know what to do with them,
                              take them to a bottle bank.

Teona Maybury (8)
Nevill Road Junior School, Bramhall

The Rainforest

With the brown bark on the bottom and the green leaves
up above,

you're taking away the things we love.
Just think of the stunning thing that came out of a seed,
you're taking away the oxygen we need.
Just hearing the chainsaw is killing me,
imagine what it's like being the poor, poor tree.
I'm seeing cut down trees everywhere, it's like I'm paranoid,
but this thing I'm seeing is impossible to avoid.
I loved what I used to see when the trees swayed,
also when the happy children played, played, played.
I look across the land and nothing is there,
no trees, no plants, no anything, everything is bare.

Chloe Buck (10)
Nine Tree Primary School, Stockbridge Village

Save Us!

Please, please help us trees
Stop before it's the end please, please my friend!

The tree stands high as the bees buzz by
I'm so sad, it's so bad.

Oh, the good old days when children played
What a wonderful world.

Now as we cower like a dog being hit
As we get chopped down bit by bit
Below me I can see a chainsaw just for me
Slowly the chainsaw comes nearer
This is the end my dear friend.

Charlie Jade Wilton (8)
Nine Tree Primary School, Stockbridge Village

Save Us!

Help us trees
we are crying
and slowly but surely dying.

Through rain and pain
through the breeze and the tease
please, please save our trees.

How the bees fly
and the animals cry
My, my, what a wonderful rainforest.

We stand as straight as soldiers
we sway in the summer breeze
but why we are our size escapes me!

Oh my, oh my big river
your colours are all bright blue
but when I come to see you
I cry the whole time through.

Hannah Mitchell (9)
Nine Tree Primary School, Stockbridge Village

Trees In The Rainforest

I remember when life was good,
I protected small mammals until it came
Until the most terrifying thing came,
It was a huge bulldozer.

I whispered to the little mouse that lived with me.
He told his friend, Mrs Bee
She told the sea
They warned the animals that lived with thee.

I was nervous until I hit the ground
Not a peep or even a sound
Now I'm gone but forever none.

Rachel Moffatt (9)
Nine Tree Primary School, Stockbridge Village

War - Haiku

Do we have to fight?
Big loud bangs all of the night
We can make it stop.

Natasha Burns (9)
Portland Primary School, Birkenhead

Pollution

P lease start using more trains
O nly use your car when you need to
L itter is dreadful, don't do it
L eave your rubbish in the bin
U se it again, don't bin it
T he trolleys are not for throwing in rivers
I know that everyone can stop polluting
O ne drug can do a lot of harm
N o one knows how much damage we are doing
   to the ozone layer.

Oliver Luke Mitchell-Shaw (7)
St George's CE Primary School, Heaviley

Recycling

If you recycle paper
It's cheaper and safer.
Recycle plastic,
To be fantastic.
Don't throw everything away,
Just start to recycle today.
Use your hands to recycle glass
And you are in top class.
Come on we can all do something
For our blue and green ball.

James Ledger (9)
St George's CE Primary School, Heaviley

Save Energy

Turn off lights when not in need,
Switch to energy-saving bulbs for a longer read.

Refill your water bottle every day,
Don't buy another one so you say.

Have a shower every night,
Don't waste water in a bath that's white.

Here's a very unusual trick,
In the back of your toilet, put a brick!

If you have a low water washing machine use it,
Otherwise use a sink to do your bit.

Bethany Jones (9)
St George's CE Primary School, Heaviley

The World Rap

Hey, the world's polluted so what are you going to do?
Hey, the animals are going away so what are you going to say?
I used to think, what's the solution to old smelly pollution?
Now it's come clear and I can see cars moving
And I can smell the fumes, oh yeah.
Now what you do is up to you so let's all have some fun.
Let's stop pollution spreading, that's where we're
heading today.

Lois White (9)
St George's CE Primary School, Heaviley

Pollution

Don't drive to school, there are too many cars,
use your bike with stars.
The A6 is a busy road, lots of lorries with heavy loads,
all the fumes make us cough and sneeze.
Come on, stop the pollution please.

Amy Worth (9)
St George's CE Primary School, Heaviley

Stop Pollution

P lease do not get in cars
O r on motorbikes
L eave the car at home
L eave the motorbike at home
U se your bike
T o get to school use your bike or walk
I nstead of using the car, take the bus
O r if you use your bike, pollution will stop
N o cars and no motorbikes means no pollution.

Lewis Parker (9)
St George's CE Primary School, Heaviley

Recycling

R ecycling is fun for everyone
E very time you recycle you help the environment
C ome on, get saving before it's too late
Y ou
C an do it
L eave the black bin outside
I n time we can make a difference
N ever put bottles in the bin
G o on, get recycling.

Katie Sandford (8)
St George's CE Primary School, Heaviley

Litter

L is for litter thrown on the streets
I is for ill sea birds poisoned by tankers' oil
T is for thick smoke polluting the air
T is for trash thrown everywhere
E is for environment being spoilt
R is for recycling to save our world.

Chloe James (8)
St George's CE Primary School, Heaviley

Endangered Animals

E ndangered animals
N eed help
D on't let them down
A nd try to help
N ever stop helping the animals
G o to the wild
E njoy the sight
R emember the animals which are
E ndangered
D on't think.

A nimals are mean, they're really
N ice
I ndeed
M ammals need help like dolphins and whales
A nd help all the pandas that
L ive in the wild
S o go out and help now.

Natasha Harford (8)
St George's CE Primary School, Heaviley

Pollution

P lease ride a bike
O r your car fumes will poison our world
L ittle by little we can make a difference
L ike don't dump your rubbish
U se a recycle bag instead
T ry to have a shower not a bath
I t may just save some water
O h, how much fun it is
N ow go and recycle!

Tyler Barker (9)
St George's CE Primary School, Heaviley

Pollution

Litter
All around us,
Pollution everywhere,
Oil and fumes, plastic and paper,
Please stop.

So think
What you're throwing,
We can make a difference,
Reduce, reuse and recycle,
Please help.

Nathan Hackney (8)
St George's CE Primary School, Heaviley

Water

Water, water everywhere
Reuse your water bottle when you drink
Water, water everywhere
Don't fill up the sink
Have a shower instead of a bath
Water, water everywhere
Don't fill up the sink.

Jordan Metcalfe (9)
St George's CE Primary School, Heaviley

Elephants - Cinquain

Hunted
For ivory
Elephants being shot
Murdered for their shiny white tusks
Helpless.

Nathan Foster (8)
St George's CE Primary School, Heaviley

Pollution

Our world
is suffering now
Pollution everywhere
it's silent and deadly
Poor world.

Our world
is suffering
because of deadly fumes
We must stop polluting
poor world.

Daniella Kinsey (9)
St George's CE Primary School, Heaviley

Pollution

Why are
the chemicals
creating pollution?
The litter and fumes destroying
our world.

Can we
save our planet?
Everyone can help to
reduce, reuse and recycle
Please help.

Kyle McKinney (9)
St George's CE Primary School, Heaviley

Stop Pollution

I hate pollution
Litter everywhere
So what's the solution?

Rubbish on every street
Blowing around
Landing on your feet.

Plastic in the sea
Oil in the ocean
I know it's up to us
To set the world free.

Daisy May Byrne (8)
St George's CE Primary School, Heaviley

Save The World!

Don't be a traitor,
just recycle paper.

If you recycle plastic
that's fantastic!

Use your hands
to recycle cans,
Go to the top of class
and recycle glass.
Don't drop the ball,
save the planet for us all.

Alan Penney (9)
St George's CE Primary School, Heaviley

Dead Or Alive?

I can see the massive puddles of rose-red blood
like a big poppy field full of beautiful poppies.

The horrific smell of puffing black smoke grasps my nose
like a nasty crab pinching my feet.

A sweet taste of happy memories grow back in my painful hand
like the one on my holiday in Spain.

Bullets firing, screams and shouts and noises from the tanks
rumbling, my head and ears are blowing up.

Gripping pain touches my poor pounding heart
like a young child begging for help and food.

Terror, lives, anger, attacks - I just can't take it anymore,
the wars have to stop!

Michael Byrne (10)
St Vincent's RC Primary School, Penketh

What I See And What I Should See

I should see bright green grass and glittery flowers
but instead I see a big muddy landfill site.

I should hear the cars being crushed but instead I hear
a huge lorry driving past to throw cans in the landfill sites.

I should taste happiness but instead I taste sadness.

I should smell the recycled fizzy drinks cans
but instead I smell oil and petrol.

I should touch and collect the garden waste
but instead I touch the rubbish bins.

I should feel joyful that everyone recycles but instead
I feel upset that quite a lot of people don't recycle.

Georgia Jones-Bale (10)
St Vincent's RC Primary School, Penketh

Joe's War

In a death I saw the blood-red mountain tops
like a bright red strawberry ice cream.
In a death I smelt the putrid stench of the smoking buildings
like a raging barbecue.
In a death I touched my brother for the last time
like letting a teddy go forever.
In a death I tasted the fear ravishing across the land
like a deadly disease.
In a death I heard the terrified people screaming
like one big siren.
In a death I felt angry, I felt weak, I felt horrid, stop it now.

Joseph Moon (11)
St Vincent's RC Primary School, Penketh

Animals

A nimals will soon start to die,
N ot unless we stop eating their thighs,
I f we do look after them they will be fine,
M y sun will start to shine,
A lligators will soon start to say their goodbyes,
L ots of newborns won't get to say hi,
S o start looking after them now!

Emma Cooney (10)
St Vincent's RC Primary School, Penketh

Endangered And Extinct

I can see animals dying like a man dying of old age.
I can hear the animals suffering like somebody being bullied.
I can taste extinction on the tip of my tongue like some
                                        foul vinegar.
I can smell the dead elephants like a slinky stink bomb.

James Cullen (10)
St Vincent's RC Primary School, Penketh

I See . . .

I see the dark grey clouds hovering over the blood-red battlefields of
the war, like a field of dancing poppies.
I see litter roaming the deserted streets like a downpour
of rain flooding our world.
I see the rainforest burning, crimson fire raging through
like an angry bull and the trees scream in fear and despair.
I see all of the animals perishing slowly like an ice lolly
in the burning hot sun.
I see the homeless families wandering around the streets
hopelessly like a cloud daydreaming across the skies.
I see the diseases looming around everyone
like the smell of my grandma's newly baked pie.
I see the money pouring out of people's lives
and becoming poor like snow falling out of the sky.
I see people laughing at the humiliated other people,
it's like a bird losing its wings.
I see the world as a better place where nothing is wrong
and everyone is happy again.

Olivia Guy (11)
St Vincent's RC Primary School, Penketh

Animal Extinction

What would happen if dolphins were extinct?
There would be no fun in the sea,
no excitement at fun parks
and no glorious sights to see.

What would happen if tigers were extinct?
There would be no terrifying and amazing shows
and no magical lives to peep in at.

What would happen if orang-utans were extinct?
There would be no terrific stunts to watch
and no funny tricks to laugh at.

Alice Durell (11)
St Vincent's RC Primary School, Penketh

Our Environment

Melting, dying, bleeding, crying in the rainforest,
Savannah and Arctic places.
I can see the icebergs tipping, breaking astray
into the endless ocean.
I can smell the boiling humidity rising
in the landscape savannah.
I can touch the scales on the dying alligator,
helpless with no water.
I can taste danger of extinction looming in the air around me.

Harry Park (11)
St Vincent's RC Primary School, Penketh

War

I can smell blood swaying through the air.
I can taste black horrible smoke choking all my friends.
I can hear all my friends screaming from the black
horrible smoke.
I can see dead bodies on the bright red poppies.
I can touch my friend's heartbeat getting slower and slower
and slower.

I feel anger burning inside me.

Thomas Lawrenson (10)
St Vincent's RC Primary School, Penketh

Fight For Life

I can see endless battlefields of blood, tears and hate.
Loud bangs and sounds of fear echo in my head.
I can smell a thick, nose-filling stench of smoke.
A bitter taste of hate and anger fills my mouth up.
I touch the dying soldiers' faces, wiping off the dirt.
I feel sad, angry, and alarmed.
The pain has to stop, this war is going to *stop!*

Monica May Nencini (9)
St Vincent's RC Primary School, Penketh

Let It End

I can see the wondrous prides of lions lying in the blazing sun
like dazzling swirls of golden sand.
The monstrous roars and shrieks of scared animals echoes
all around me like the horrific shouts of the dreadful poachers
as they catch their prey.
I can taste the hatred and sadness in the scorching jungle
like a never-ending memory of all the loyal animals that were
taken by the fearsome hunters.
The shiny and smooth ivory tusk crawls through my palm
like a graceful dancer twirling round my fingers.
Horror, disgust, outrage! It needs to stop, leave the animals in peace.

Katie Garvey (11)
St Vincent's RC Primary School, Penketh

Emotional

I can see the people queuing for ages, like writing
covering up pages
Gas lingers up my nose, as planes pass in the rain flows.
Pain bangs on my chest, there isn't very much left.
The taste of fear creeps up my arm, as dying bodies
clear the farms.

Boom, bang, it feels like the end,
Upset, worried, scared.

Juliet Porter (10)
St Vincent's RC Primary School, Penketh

My War Poem

I can see the red blood leaking out of people's bodies
while they are in pain.
I can feel the cold breeze on my fingertips cooling my body.
I can hear the screaming voices looming around my head.
I can taste the black smoky fire making my eyes go fuzzy.
I can smell all of the rotten bodies all around me.

Rachael Keoghan (10)
St Vincent's RC Primary School, Penketh

The Elephant

I stomped across the ground, my feet were aching,
I was covered in cuts and bruises.
My family have a disease, no one comes to help us,
Death was on our shoulders, my life at risk.
I could see the cage, the cage my family were trapped in,
Disturbed to see this sight.
My family were driven away,
Down the road near the bay.
Abused when I was young,
My owner was beaten and hung.
What can I do now?
I cannot eat the grass while the grass is dead.
Not only is the grass dead, it's covered in blood-red.
I am all alone, I need some help.
Can you be the person who will help?

Michael Manning (11)
St Vincent's RC Primary School, Penketh

Cruelty - Lion

I am sat lonely in an abandoned forest watching my friends
be shot for our splendid mane and fur.
I can smell the burning bonfire glistening in the moonlight.
My elegant mane is waving in the dark sky.
I can feel the gentle long strides of grass
waiting slowly for the spring.
I can taste fear upon me as I say goodbye
to my friends and family.
I can hear trucks driving, driving away,
taking all we have away from us.
My elegant mane shakes as I try to
take my mind off the hunters.
I can hear my life ticking away, I'm next.

Alice Clarke (10)
St Vincent's RC Primary School, Penketh

The City War . . .

In a city I saw
Death and war . . .
The danger and sadness
And no smiling or gladness.
I hear the screams from below,
Innocent soldiers dying row by row.
As we escape I touch in my hands,
The rough crumbly rocks upon the beach sands.
I smell the stench of rotting corpses,
Stood by them their faithful horses.
People can taste the cold salty air,
The breeze blowing through everyone's hair.
The mood in my head is angry and sad,
All of this *war* makes me *mad!*

Olivia Rudkin (11)
St Vincent's RC Primary School, Penketh

War, War

War, war is a terrible thing,
War, war, the screaming men,
War, war, the alive men fall,
War, war is a gruesome thing.

War, war is a horrible thing,
War, war, the blood of men,
War, war, the loud guns firing,
War, war is a very sad thing.

War, war is a brutal thing,
War, war, the retreating men run,
War, war, will it ever end?
War, war is a nasty thing.

Callum Teeling (10)
St Vincent's RC Primary School, Penketh

Rainforest Destruction

Rainforest, rainforest with oak trees,
Rainforest, rainforest losing its trees,
Rainforest, rainforest with buzzing bees,
Rainforest, rainforest, where are those bees?

Rainforest, rainforest, look at those tigers,
Rainforest, rainforest, here come the hunters,
Rainforest, rainforest, how the deer tan,
Rainforest, rainforest, here comes Man.

Rainforest, rainforest, that's a big paw,
Rainforest, rainforest, there's a chainsaw,
Rainforest, rainforest, down goes the moon,
Rainforest, rainforest come back soon.

Jordan Matthew Newall (10)
St Vincent's RC Primary School, Penketh

Poachers

I should see the elephants playing in the water,
but I see a muddy swamp empty.
I should hear the lions roaring in the sun,
but I hear a deadly silence.
I should touch the soft silky fur of a polar bear
but instead I just touch the icy water.
I should smell the rhinos doing their business
but I smell the poachers' petrol.
I should taste the sea near the elegant dolphins
but I taste a terrible bitter taste.
I should feel happy that the animals are strolling around me
but instead I feel sad that everything is quiet.

Tilly Hemsley (10)
St Vincent's RC Primary School, Penketh

My Dream!

I am the Earth, twirling around at a slow pace.
I feel the sun getting through my layer of protection.
It is hurting, making a hole in my protection.
Beating down on the icebergs, melting is what they are doing.

My dream is for the world to be a cheerful place,
All the countries are friends with each other,
The children playing, people using the transport that only uses
a bit of fuel,
No fighting, no war, that is my dream.

But instead it is not at all true, my dream of my dream coming true
is never going to happen.
The world is a harmful place, fighting, war, climate change
We need to change it, the harmful rays are melting the icebergs
We will eventually be underwater, I can see it now . . .

The water, the fear of children and adults is a piercing sound,
deafening screams,
I can taste fear rushing around the world,
I feel the water gushing against my skin.
I can smell the gases and the sea salt running up my nostrils.
My eyes are picturing terrible sights, people, families running
for safety,
Maybe . . . just maybe if we start to do something, my dream
will come true.

Emily Moriarty (11)
St Vincent's RC Primary School, Penketh

Wild War

B attle should be banned, it is no way to fight,
A t any moment a war can be declared,
T all with lots of guns, that's an army tank,
T alented soldiers always walk home untouched,
L ying down dead, sad, terror, death,
E legant as that sounds, it's not.

Hayley Houghton (10)
St Vincent's RC Primary School, Penketh

War

I can see the madness and hatred in the enemy's dark,
angry eyes.
I can see the bloody fields of death with dancing poppies
blowing in the wind.
I can hear the screaming, the explosions, the fear in their voices.
I can hear the deadly silence in the air.
I can hear the footsteps of the enemy patrol.
I can hear the voices of my parents' last lost words.
I can smell the blood running through the valleys
Like raindrops drizzling down a window.
I can smell the fear of everyone around me,
Not knowing whether they'll live or die.
I can feel the crippling pain touch my heart like a small child
Lying in an empty landscape . . . dying on his own.
I can taste the anger in my throat, as I witness another
horrific death.

Sadness, anger, terror, fear, hatred!
It has to stop *now!*

Jack Lavan (11)
St Vincent's RC Primary School, Penketh

Racism

My friends have left me because they are so scared.
I don't know how this is going to end.
I didn't ask for a perfect life
So could you please stop bullying me.
I am so scared of what you will do to me,
That's why I am so late for school.
I'm scared to tell anyone that I'm getting bullied
So please stop soon.
I'm getting worried, it is because of you that I have nightmares
So please stop soon, the nightmares are getting worse.

Jessica Alexander (9)
St Vincent's RC Primary School, Penketh

The Life Poem

Save the rainforests and the trees,
Save the animals and buzzy bees.

Different coloured people should be treated the same,
Otherwise life wouldn't be a fair game.

Try recycling, it is cool,
Polluting the Earth is really cruel.

Save the ozone by not using a car
And our life will go on far.

Try not to litter, it is bad,
Try to recycle it is rad.

Stop the war in Iraq,
Tell all the soldiers to come back.

Josh Newton (10)
St Vincent's RC Primary School, Penketh

Suffering Creatures

As I lay there trapped, cold, scared and injured
And death in every corner,
I couldn't help take in my surroundings.
I couldn't do anything, I was trapped.
As I lay there waiting for death,
Memories flashed through my head of the good days
When man and animal were good friends.
Now I'm lying here watching my home get ripped apart
By the monstrous beasts we call humans.
The stench of rotting flesh and blood powered over
The sweet scent of blossom trees and flowers.
Bodies lie on the floor surrounded by pools of blood.

Rubie Maiy Edgar (11)
St Vincent's RC Primary School, Penketh

Alex's War

I can see puddles of red-rose blood
But not many soldiers stood.
Pain, screaming, dying like an exploding bomb
                              terrorising the city.
I can taste hatred on the tip of my tongue like a rotten apple.
Terrorising pain touches my heart like Cupid's arrow.
I can smell the putrid smoke like my dad's
                              smouldering barbecue.
Anger! Pain! Disgust! Outrage!
Save them! Save everyone!

Alex Buckley (11)
St Vincent's RC Primary School, Penketh

Homeless!

Being homeless is very bad,
this makes me very sad.
We have no money because we are poor,
we cannot afford to clean the floor.
When we have no food,
this puts me in a big bad mood.
We all have very dirty feet
and we cannot afford to eat.
I really wish I had a home
so then I wouldn't feel alone.

Imogen Walker (9)
St Wilfrid's CE Primary School, Grappenhall

The Big Green Poetry Machine

The big green poetry machine
Helping the world go truly green
Power plants and stations will soon all be gone
Roses, tulips, there will be none.

Lara Flannery (10)
St Wilfrid's CE Primary School, Grappenhall

Let's Save The World

If we make the world a better place,
you'll see more smiles on a child's face.
Clean up all the mess and litter,
then the Earth won't be so bitter.
Let's clean up and make the Earth cleaner,
if we stay together we'll make the world greener.
Mess and litter, keep it clean,
then we could have a world that's green.
Recycle waste to protect pollution,
like car fumes, rubbish and exhaustion.
If you walk instead of drive,
you could be keeping people alive.

Hannah Jackson (10)
St Wilfrid's CE Primary School, Grappenhall

Homeless

Please help the children
That do not have homes
And some of the children are alone

Children really want a warm home
Instead of living on the streets without anyone
No mum, dad, sister or brothers.

Nicola Hilton (9)
St Wilfrid's CE Primary School, Grappenhall

Litter

Litter, litter, what a shame
It's everywhere, I do complain
That the environment is lame
Next time you drop litter
You will get a fine.

Ruby Jude Kelly (8)
St Wilfrid's CE Primary School, Grappenhall

Eco-Friendly

Eco-friendly
Eco-safe
Eco is my favourite place
Friendly flowers
Friendly trees
Buildings are disgusting things
Rubbish bins are for your litter
The smell of car fumes so horrid, so bitter
So I would like to show a difference
Today will be better than any other day
And sadly I have no other way.

Charlotte Capper (10)
St Wilfrid's CE Primary School, Grappenhall

Recycle

R educe, reuse, recycle
E nvironment matters the most
C an you help keep our world green?
Y ou can recycle anything
C ans, clothes, everything helps
L ittle things still make a difference
E very little helps.

Katie Butler (9)
St Wilfrid's CE Primary School, Grappenhall

Recycling

Recycle your waste paper
It will go a long way
Cos if everyone recycled
Their waste today
Then we would have more trees
Making our world a nicer place to be.

Liam Gray (9)
St Wilfrid's CE Primary School, Grappenhall

Our World

People who are homeless, they live on the street
and every day they walk on their bare feet
They find food out of bins
and eat out of horrible tins
Everyone needs to recycle their paper
so it will be a lot safer
People use gas
and they should have a pass
This is our world.

Megan Dunbavand (10)
St Wilfrid's CE Primary School, Grappenhall

Plants

I was once in the street looking at my feet
and I saw a tree that was as big as my knee
I had not seen one of those before
so I left it be

I saw a flower
It was not as big as a tower
but it was a flower and it's got power.

Cameron McLay (9)
St Wilfrid's CE Primary School, Grappenhall

Recycle!

R educe, reuse, recycle!
E mpty bottles into the bottle bank
C are for the world
Y ou can recycle most materials
C an you recycle?
L itter is bad for the world
E very little helps!

Charlotte Day (9)
St Wilfrid's CE Primary School, Grappenhall

Recycle

R ecycle your paper
E nvironment, keep care of the environment
C are for our world
Y ou can recycle paper, card, cardboard, glass, plastic,
    clothes, bottles and cans
C an you help us stay green?
L itter, you can't drop litter on the floor otherwise
    you will get charged
E very little helps!

Matt Barker (10)
St Wilfrid's CE Primary School, Grappenhall

Recycle

R ecycle and things can be used again.
E nvironment is important to keep clean.
C are to our world will make a nicer place.
Y ou can recycle items such as paper, glass and many more.
C an you help us stay green?
L ittering is against the law.
E very little thing could help.

Jacob Wilkinson (10)
St Wilfrid's CE Primary School, Grappenhall

The Earth

It used to be so bright and fun
But now the trouble has just begun,
Where trees once stood and plants grew high,
There are now tall buildings that reach the sky,
It doesn't have to be this way,
So why not recycle every day?

Darcey Brooks (9)
St Wilfrid's CE Primary School, Grappenhall

Eco Race

It's a race
To make the world a better place,
To recycle
And cycle
To school
Or work.
It's a race
To make the world a better place,
To stop global warming,
Animal extinction,
Disease,
War,
It's all in our hands.
It's a race
To make the world a better place.

Jodie Williams (11)
St Wilfrid's CE Primary School, Grappenhall

Homeless

If you have no home,
you might feel alone,
if you've got no food,
then you could be in a bad mood.

You might eat out of a bin,
you might eat carrots from a tin,
or because you're poor
you might eat off the floor.

You might not have many
maybe only one penny,
you might have holes
as big as moles
in your clothes.

Daniel Evans (10)
St Wilfrid's CE Primary School, Grappenhall

Homeless

You don't feel very well
because of the smell,
unlike you and me
there's no one to tell.
You really want something new
but there's nothing to do.
You have a big frown
that gets everybody down.
There's nobody to phone
and you haven't got a home.
You live on the street
and you don't know who you will meet.
You feel really sad
when you've been bad.
Would you like to be homeless?

Lucy Bennison (10)
St Wilfrid's CE Primary School, Grappenhall

Lousy Litter

Here, there, everywhere
Comes lots of lousy litter,
In the park,
In the river,
Lots of lousy litter.

In the sea,
In the streets
Lots of lousy litter.
Bottles in the bottle bank,
Papers in the paper bin,
Plastic in the plastic box,
That's how to deal with litter.

Cameron Elizabeth Nyland (8)
St Wilfrid's CE Primary School, Grappenhall

If We Didn't Recycle

If we didn't recycle
The world would be full of cans
The air would be polluted
By cars, planes and vans.

If we didn't recycle
There would be no more ice
For polar bears and penguins
It will not be very nice.

If we didn't recycle
There would be no place to play
Because of all the landfill
All the parks would go away.

Let all this be a warning
Recycling must be done
To help save the planet
And it can be fun.

Maddie Hardern (8)
St Wilfrid's CE Primary School, Grappenhall

It's Hard When You're On The Streets

It's hard when you're on the streets,
There is not even a crumb to eat.

All of my horrible raggy clothes
Have gigantic holes.

All you do is moan and groan
And think about your luxurious dream home.

The horrible everyday smell
Makes you feel really unwell.

I pray to have a home and look up to the sky,
Every day I hope, and cry and cry.

Olivia Thompson (9)
St Wilfrid's CE Primary School, Grappenhall

Stay Green

Racism is red,
War is blue
And they are both as thick as the end of my shoe.

Climate change can kill the world
And then we will be as dead as dust.
Then there is litter,
That is plain lazy.

Disease makes you dead
And homelessness makes you have no bed,
Pollution is bad
And poverty is sad.

I hope that we can make a change
And the world will stop being strange.

Jacob Mark Nolan (10)
St Wilfrid's CE Primary School, Grappenhall

Our Planet

Save our planet, help us . . .
Reduce
Reuse
Recycle.
Give away your kindness today
and it might start to help in a very special way.
Our world is special so we should reduce our rubbish
in every good way.
Don't neglect your rubbish, it might affect our planet.
So . . . help us now to reduce our affects
and keep away from rubbish - protect!
If it carries on this way,
our lives will be filled with dismay.

Rosie Walton Ryder (10)
St Wilfrid's CE Primary School, Grappenhall

Life

Tiger and mouse,
Without a home and without a house,
Poverty and poorness,
A smile and a frown,
With a little care and love, we could turn this world around.

War and peace,
Up and down,
Happiness and litter on the ground.
Disease and health
Poor and wealth.

Think of a world without laughter, a smile
Or a polar bear in the wild,
Think of a world where the ice caps have melted,
Think of a world without war, pain or death,
So let's walk to school and travel by train.

Think of the soldiers marched to their death,
Imagine you were taking your last breath,
Think of the children starving in Africa,
If only the world would get along and not bicker.
All it takes is a little time and consideration,
All we have to do is use our concentration.

Sarah Hewitt (10)
St Wilfrid's CE Primary School, Grappenhall

Save The Planet!

Nick's big green thing to pollution,
If we all work together we'll think of a solution.
Hop on the bus, don't make a fuss
And remember to hold onto the bars.
So just hop on, whilst you eat a scone
Because buses hold over forty cars.
Everyone pick up the litter, your mum, your dad,
Or maybe your babysitter,
To save the planet Earth!

Maddie Smetham (9)
St Wilfrid's CE Primary School, Grappenhall

Opposites

Black or white,
Rude or polite,
Pollution or fresh air,
Animals that are becoming extinct like a polar bear.
Smile or frown,
Litter on the ground,
Paper or trees,
Ashes or leaves,
Smoke or mist,
High five or fist,
Handicapped or clown,
Feeling happy or feeling down.
These are some opposites that cause chaos in life,
So let's put an end to this silly old strife,
Pick up some litter, stop torturing trees, walk instead of drive and
                                                    sweep up the leaves.
By following these simple chores the world can become
                                                    a better place
And that means a great big smile upon your face.

Olivia Lloyd (10)
St Wilfrid's CE Primary School, Grappenhall

The World

The park used to be bright and fun,
but now the trouble has just begun.
Why are we treating the world this way?
because now children can no longer play.

The birds in the world sing many a song,
now let's leave them where they belong.
We can live without the meat,
I don't think we should even have it for a treat.

Now let's not drive so many cars
And stop smoking, even in bars.

Lydia Marrable (9)
St Wilfrid's CE Primary School, Grappenhall

Go Green Guys

'Go green guys,' said Billy Joe, 'see there's no more
winter snow.'
The guys all laughed and looked away.
'Guys come back, oh please just stay, do you know why there's no
more snow? Because people are bad to the planet you know.'

But you can help by turning off your lights when there is nobody
in the room
and you can help by turning off the tap when you aren't washing
your hands,
and why put stuff in the bin when you can just recycle?

So have a go and you will see next year will be more fun
because of all the work we've done.

Jessica Street (9)
St Wilfrid's CE Primary School, Grappenhall

Recycle

Recycling may seem difficult but it's easy really
And you may find it hard at first but you love Earth clearly
At first it won't come naturally but over time it will
Plus we will pay the price when we see all that it will kill
But we have our ups and we have our downs
And we have our friends and turn around
But even if we're feeling sad
That's no reason to be bad
So help recycle everywhere
And show the world that you care.

Eve Johnstone (10)
St Wilfrid's CE Primary School, Grappenhall

Imagine . . .

Imagine if . . . it snowed in the desert and the Antarctic
had a blazing sun.
If we had no pandas or polar bears, it wouldn't be much fun.
What if the rainforest had no trees and if our world
was covered in wars?
If England was knee-deep in litter, like tin cans and apple cores.
Imagine if the world was like this because you know
it actually could.
If we're not wise and don't recycle, we could have no paper
or wood.
But if we recycle the world could stay green and blue.
I know I'm going to recycle, I hope you are too.

Lucy Massey (9)
St Wilfrid's CE Primary School, Grappenhall

If I Could Make The World Change

If I could make the world change all the pollution would go
There would be tweeting birds and a bright blue sky
All the flowers would grow
Easter would come sooner
Then every child could play catch.
Mother chick would be singing to her eggs
Come on babies, hatch, hatch, hatch
At the end of spring everyone would sing from the joy summer
would bring
At the start of autumn the leaves would fall from the trees
so very tall.

Millie Johnson (7)
St Wilfrid's CE Primary School, Grappenhall

Earth

Litter, war, rainforest, disease
People losing their families.
Please stop doing these dreadful deeds
And help the world and its needs.
Motorbike, car, bus, plane,
All make the Earth complain.

Racism, extinction, death and more,
Should never have been discovered before.
Car fumes and factory smoke, aren't very nice.
They disagree with the environment's right.

Make these things history
And let the world live in harmony
And become an eco-warrior.

Jimmy Ashcroft (9)
St Wilfrid's CE Primary School, Grappenhall

Extinction

Racism is red
Being homeless is blue
And they are both as sick as my auntie's shoe
Recycling is good
But you could do better giving or buying from charity.

Animals' homes are being cut down
Thinking of that just makes me frown
The rainforest will die if you don't just try
If you start recycling then you will be rewarded
In your own special way.

Simon Roberts (9)
St Wilfrid's CE Primary School, Grappenhall

Extinction

One day there was lots
the next there was none
polar bears are none
rabbits are lots.

Golden eagles are none
dogs are lots
honey badgers are none
cats are lots.

Animals are losing their homes
with hunters after their skins
humans don't give help
just make it worse!

Ross McKinnon (10)
St Wilfrid's CE Primary School, Grappenhall

Let's Go Green

Save the planet by going green
get rid of litter and keep it clean
Let's all recycle, stop littering
and all be part of the big green thing
Why don't we all stop pollution
like rubbish waste and car exhaustion
The plants are dying
animals are getting extinct
so let's be good and let's be green.

Nicole Kelly (9)
St Wilfrid's CE Primary School, Grappenhall

Homeless

It's hard when you're homeless,
all you can do is moan and groan.
It's hard when you're on the street,
When all day long you're on your feet.
It's hard when you're poor
and both of your feet are really sore.
It's hard when you have to look in the bin
and all you can find is a rusty tin.
It's hard when you don't have any money
And all the time you miss luxuries like honey.

Rebecca Mitchell (10)
St Wilfrid's CE Primary School, Grappenhall

Wars Kill - Cinquain

Dead men
Death caused by war
Innocent die all day
Stop wars, wars, oh terrible wars
Wars kill.

Henry James Simpson (9)
St Wilfrid's CE Primary School, Grappenhall

Remember

R emember the world can't last forever
E xtinction of the planet
C limate change can kill the world
Y ou can make a difference
C an you make the world a better place? Yes you can
L ive your life the right way
I know we can make a change
N ow's the time to help
G et recycling.

Eleanor Pink (10)
St Wilfrid's CE Primary School, Grappenhall

Eco-Kids

Save our environment
Eco, eco-kids
Don't dump stuff in the bin
Eco, eco-kids
Rainforests cut down
Eco, eco-kids and friends
Big wars
Eco, eco-kids and nature
Extinct animals
I want to help
Being homeless and refugees
Eco helps
Diseases
Help us fans
Eco, eco-kids
I'm an eco-kid!

Libby Richardson (7)
St Wilfrid's CE Primary School, Grappenhall

Be Green!

R ainforests
E xtinction
C limate change
Y ou're in control
C ollect
L itter
I ndifference
N ow you are harming our planet
G et changing.

Isobel McGann (10)
St Wilfrid's CE Primary School, Grappenhall

Recycling

R ecycling should be
E verlasting and takes great
C are
Y ou
C an recycle
L oads of things
I magine
N o
G arbage!

Kyle Reed (10)
Woodchurch Road Primary School, Oxton

War

S ave innocent people from war,
T oo many people die from it,
O ur Earth is at risk,
P rotect the world, stop wars now.

W hy do we have war?
A peaceful world? That sounds good.
R id the world of war.

Isabel Nolan (10)
Woodchurch Road Primary School, Oxton

Litter

L ife
I s
T errible
T reating
E verything as
R ubbish.

Olivia Hulmston (10)
Woodchurch Road Primary School, Oxton

Pollution

P lease love your Earth
O nly you can make the right choice
L ove nature
L ittering can cause pollution
U nless we act things will get worse
T ake the opportunity to clean the Earth
I f you don't things will get worse
O nly we can do it
N ever kill lives.

Georgina Bryan-Owens (10)
Woodchurch Road Primary School, Oxton

War

W ar, what is it good for?
A bsolutely nothing.
R acism is bad, stop it now.

I raq is at war at the moment,
S ave innocent people.

B ombs and weapons are killing people,
A rmy troops are helping out,
D eath is evil, stop it now.

Christopher Chan (10)
Woodchurch Road Primary School, Oxton

Litter

L ots of rubbish
I n our town
T ogether we can beat it
T hrow it all in bins
E arth needs our help
R ecycle!

Kyle Burgess (10)
Woodchurch Road Primary School, Oxton

Bird Overhead

Bird overhead, what do you see?
Plastic bags blowing in the breeze.
Seagulls scavenging for food,
Polystyrene blowing like snow.
A massive bulldozer moving like a snail,
Smooth, shiny cans crushed by feet.
A tyre like a massive doughnut,
Paper blowing away in the breeze.
Boxes rolling across the landfill,
What a waste!

Ewan Nolan (8)
Woodchurch Road Primary School, Oxton

Earth's Destruction

Polluting is bad
Because people are mad
And people aren't glad
That they're sad
That the Earth is dying
And the ozone's frying
There's so much madness
So make some gladness.

Ewan McVey (10)
Woodchurch Road Primary School, Oxton

Animal Extinction

Animals are not toys.
Animals should not be killed for pleasure
So give them their leisure.

Shaun Jones (10)
Woodchurch Road Primary School, Oxton

Animal Extinction

Animal extinction means endangered species
And that means they die and that is not a lie.
Some are healthy, some are not,
Loads die, well not the lot.
Some suffocate, some can't breathe,
But with their family they have to leave,
Into the grave they go
And they sink into the ground deep down below.
They can't live forever
And the answer to that would be never, never, never!

Ashley Kay (10)
Woodchurch Road Primary School, Oxton

Rainforests

Don't make wildlife suffer,
Just to make us tougher.
Animals are in danger, can't you see?
It's just making our lives bad for you and me.
Trees are getting chopped down,
Soon there will be none left in the town.
Don't throw litter on the ground,
Recycle rubbish and make it go around.

Nathan Boult (9)
Woodchurch Road Primary School, Oxton

Litter Is All Around Us

Litter is everywhere
Some people don't really care
They're not aware
So please everyone can you care?
Stop being a litterbug out there
Use the bins, that's why they're there.

Chantelle Davies (10)
Woodchurch Road Primary School, Oxton

Bird's Eye View

Birds overhead, what do you see?
Plastic bags blowing in the breeze
Seagulls scavenging for food
Bulldozers as slow as a snail
Cans and boxes that could be recycled
Paper blowing
Tyres lying like huge black doughnuts
Polystyrene like snow
What a waste!

Summer Gleave (7) & Gabrielle Pritchard (8)
Woodchurch Road Primary School, Oxton

What A Waste!

Bird overhead, what do you see?
Plastic bags swishing in the wind.
Seagulls scavenging for wasted food,
A bulldozer creeping like a snail.
Cans being crushed by feet,
Boxes melting like ice by the rain,
Tyres shaped like giant doughnuts,
What a waste!

Cerys Owen (8)
Woodchurch Road Primary School, Oxton

Our World

The world is in trouble, we need to help it,
We need to help the trees because trees give us paper,
Stop polluting our Earth,
It is killing lots of animals, we need to help the animals,
Stop throwing rubbish in the sea,
It lies in your destiny to save
And care for the world.

Luke Price (9)
Woodchurch Road Primary School, Oxton

Pollution

P onds are not bins
O il slicks are hazards
L itter kills wildlife
L et people be free from pollution
U nderstand no one likes pollution
T hink about it
I magine being a tiny creature dying because of pollution
O ur world as well, not just yours
N ever make pollution.

Connor Weston (9)
Woodchurch Road Primary School, Oxton

Pollution

P ollution is bad,
O ur world is sad,
L isten to your heart,
L isten to the beat,
U se a different place and dump it in the bin,
T o help the animals out at sea,
I n your heart you are helpful and kind,
O n the top of the water helpless fish die for no reason,
N o one should dump pollution.

Emma Langhorn (9)
Woodchurch Road Primary School, Oxton

Litter

Litter is all around us
and some people aren't aware
So please can you care and not pollute the air
because pollution isn't fair.

Rebekah Jane Smith (10)
Woodchurch Road Primary School, Oxton

Our World

P ollution is bad,
O ur aim is to be glad,
L iving in our world is scary,
L ess airy,
U nderstand the ozone layer is running out,
T ime is running down,
I ll children in the world,
O xygen is running,
N o more polluting.

Jessica Jones (10)
Woodchurch Road Primary School, Oxton

Our World

Our world is a wonderful place,
If you don't clean it up it will be a disgrace,
People pollute all the time,
But don't do it because it is a crime.

Our world is a beautiful land,
Keep it clean, keep it grand,
Living in our world is frightening
Because the ozone layer is breaking.

Ellen Allinson
Woodchurch Road Primary School, Oxton

Pick It Up

Watch the litter fall night and day
Sometimes it never goes away
Use the bins, that's good
Don't just drop it in the mud.

Olivia Asterley (10)
Woodchurch Road Primary School, Oxton

Litter Is Bad

Litter is bad,
The world is less glad.
Don't throw litter on the floor,
Pollution will come more.
Plants will die
And the world will fry.

Global warming is coming nearer,
Come on, clean up,
Help the world survive
This terrible bumpy ride.

Don't waste time,
Don't ignore this rhyme,
Help the world by cleaning,
Please understand this meaning.

Emily Norris (9)
Woodchurch Road Primary School, Oxton

The Horror Of War

War is bad, the deaths are sad,
thinking about it just makes me mad.

All the darkness follows every war
changing the world into a bore.
Sadness whistles through the air
making the streets go bare.

Red water flows throughout the street
making its way around the feet.

Thomas Wynne (10)
Woodchurch Road Primary School, Oxton

Bird Overhead, What Do You See?

Bird overhead, what do you see?
Plastic bags blowing in the breeze.
The screeching seagulls scavenging for lunch,
A huge bulldozer creeping slowly like a caterpillar.
A big black tyre like a doughnut lying on the rubbish,
A piece of polystyrene blowing in the light breeze like snow.
Smooth, shiny cans crunching under people's feet,
Cardboard boxes rolling down the dump like tumbling weeds.
What a waste!

Chloe Griffiths (8)
Woodchurch Road Primary School, Oxton

Recycling

R euse and recycle
E nergy is important so save it
C are for the world and care for our country
Y ou have a part to play
C arefully putting stuff in the right bin
L ook out for people who don't recycle
I believe you can make a difference
N ow help us along the path to recycling
G lobal warming is coming, so hurry up and recycle.

Suzie Gray (10)
Woodchurch Road Primary School, Oxton

Litter

L et the world be a happy place,
I t will not ever be a disgrace,
T ell the people to pick up litter,
T ell the world to not be bitter,
E njoy and please don't destroy,
R espect the world, it's not a toy.

Joseph McGeoch (10)
Woodchurch Road Primary School, Oxton

Stop Bullying

B ullying is bad,
U nderstanding why they do it we will never know,
L ove people to make them happy,
L earn to understand,
Y ou can stop the bullies so why not do it?
I feel so lonely all the time,
N ever bully ever again,
G o, you know you can stop all the bullies in the world.

Alex Price (9)
Woodchurch Road Primary School, Oxton

Endangered World

Leaves and plants bring joy to the world,
Forests and rainforests a tropical wonder.
Animals and insects roaming the trees,
Poachers and woodcutters killing and chopping down forests.
Beautiful animals endangered every second,
The ozone layer destroyed and broken every day.

Ashley Dempsey (10)
Woodchurch Road Primary School, Oxton

Stop War

War kills people,
War isn't fair.
Why everybody? Don't you care?
Bombs explode,
Guns reload,
Stop war now!
Stop it for good,
Everybody come back to your neighbourhood.

Lara Jones (10)
Woodchurch Road Primary School, Oxton

Wild World

Animals live on our land
But they're not feeling grand
Think about animals in the wild
Calling a message to their child.

Turtles in the sea
Don't jump with glee
Let the fishes swim fast
The sea creatures might last.

The tundras are very cold but getting hot
The mother's babies hiding in their cot
As the Arctic releases its gale
The tundra animals aren't wiggling their tails.

Clark Isaac Morton (10)
Woodchurch Road Primary School, Oxton

Our World

Our world is a lovely place
so why do people make it a disgrace?
Come on people - wake up,
why don't you brighten the place up?
Our world is turning bad and people are getting mad.
Please make me better so I won't be a disgrace.
Our world is beginning to die,
so don't let time fly by.
As you know the world is sad,
so please make it very glad.

Casey Stanley (10)
Woodchurch Road Primary School, Oxton

Our Garbage Bin

Sometimes I think of the world as a giant garbage bin,
Where people throw things like bottles of gin.
People meet in the street, laugh and joke,
Then throw cans of Coke.

Pollution these days
Could be stopped in so many ways,
If only we could figure out what they are,
Like not using our car.
Think,
Don't let the world shrink -
Just think!

Then maybe some day,
If we have it our way,
The world will be clean
And our ideas will no longer be a dream . . .

Eleanor Gray (10)
Woodlands Primary School, Formby

Litter

Once there was a boy called Jim
Who regularly committed a sin -
Dropped his litter on the floor
Which then blew through the neighbour's door.

Next door lived a boy called Bill
Who never committed a sin -
Always walked to the bin,
Each time got fitter
Never left Mother Nature litter.

Henry Thomas Evans (9)
Woodlands Primary School, Formby

Footprints

There used to be so many,
Of the world's footprints to see,
We thought it was a nuisance,
But now we know it was lovely.

You see, when we use vehicles
And oily, smoky cars,
We are driving, not walking,
So the only footprints left are Tar's.

If the whole of our population
Could wake up and understand,
The ozone layer would be perfect,
Also very, very grand.

So why not R R R:
Recycle,
Reuse . . .
Erm . . .
Save the world!

Jessica Howlett (10)
Woodlands Primary School, Formby

Save! - Haiku

You can save the Earth,
You can save the Earth with me -
Come on, it is fun.

Lauren MacGregor (9)
Woodlands Primary School, Formby

Don't Use The Car!

Don't use the car
Wherever you are.
Take a big hike,
Get on your bike.

Go for a jog,
Don't sit like a log.
Go for a run,
Have fun in the sun.

Go for a trot,
Make the most of the muscles you've got.
Have a fast scoot,
It will be such a hoot.

Take a fast walk,
You may see a hawk.
Go for a swim,
Or workout in the gym.

You will be healthy
And possibly more wealthy.
Don't use the car
And be a superstar.

Alexander Uffendell (9)
Woodlands Primary School, Formby

We All Stand Together

As we drive round in our Mercedes-Benz
Just take a thought of all those lives that have come to an end
The earthquake in China, the hurricane in Burma
Do you think about what they're eating tonight as you bite
your burger?

It's times such as these when we should all unite
To help those people in the dead of the night
Come rain or shine no matter the weather
We all stand together.

Families, friends, pets and pictures of treasured memories,
These people lost it all
Due to global warming we all contribute
Now we've come to this brick wall
So stop all war, put guns down
There are people out there who need our help now
So hear their cry, hear their call
We need to all stand tall.

So let's stand together and help all those people
Rebuilding their towns, villages and homes
It's going to take lots of time and effort
But all together we can do it
Rain or shine, no matter the weather
We will all stand together.

Lois Diane Hardman (9)
Woodlands Primary School, Formby

Young Writers Information

We hope you have enjoyed reading this book - and that you will continue to enjoy it in the coming years.

If you like reading and writing poetry drop us a line, or give us a call, and we'll send you a free information pack.

Alternatively if you would like to order further copies of this book or any of our other titles, then please give us a call or log onto our website at www.youngwriters.co.uk

**Young Writers Information
Remus House
Coltsfoot Drive
Peterborough
PE2 9JX**

(01733) 890066